I0832281

PURELY WANNA BE

Like Jesus

By Marivic "Vic" Gillooley

Books may be ordered through booksellers or by contacting:
Marivic "Vic" Gillooley
vicgilwisdom15@gmail.com

Raising The Standard International Publishing LLC
E-Book ISBN- 9781960641960
Printed in the United States of America
Edition Date: March 2026

Table of Contents

	Acknowledgments	
	Introduction—I Wanna Be…	1
1	With God, All Is Possible	6
2	Memories	10
3	Peace	14
4	The Talk	18
5	Calling God In Troubled Times	22
6	Your Basic Identity: Your Name	26
7	The Power Of Touch	32
8	Just In Time	37
9	Safe Travels	41
10	Your Words	45
11	Go The Distance	50
12	Warrior, Worrier	55
13	The Armor	59
14	Don't Quit	63
15	Good Morning!	67
16	Grateful And Grumbling	70
17	Who Wants To Be Second	74

18 Count On It 80

19 Go The Extra Mile 84

20 Bring The Light, Be The Light 88

21 Your Circle Matters 93

22 Clean Me Up Inside 97

23 Fishing Lessons 102

24 I'm Done 106

Conclusion 111

Bibliography

About The Author

Acknowledgements

I am deeply grateful to all who have been part of this journey—whether directly or indirectly—inspiring the words of this book. From my earliest walk with Jesus until today, you have shaped, encouraged, and blessed me in countless ways.

Jen—You started everything! Your invitation and your warm, welcoming family connected me to Christ. I am forever thankful for your mentorship. You led me to Jesus and expanded my family through our very first small group, which built a strong and lasting friendship with Chrissy and her family—complete with late-night talks and endless laughter.

Lori—More than a great friend, you are a patient and gifted editor. You have edited many of my school papers, but this one…I am especially grateful for. Your expertise, insight, and encouragement have been a true gift.

Jody and family—Jody, thank you for always pursuing our friendship. Our early morning walks and prayers have shaped me more than you know. You inspire me to serve and to walk with the Lord as faithfully as you do.

Chrissy—Your friendship has blessed me and my family more than you know. Your servant's heart has challenged me, encouraged me, and held me accountable in my walk with the Lord. I'm truly grateful for you.

Ines—What a stranger to a friend and now family. Our relationship has grown so deep in the Lord, it feels weird when we miss our long, late-night phone calls that always end in a sweet Jesus-praising session. Thank you for your input. Praising the Lord with me as I shared the process of this book.

Sheila—Our friendship of over 30 years—spanning college days and so many chapters of life—has been one of God's sweetest gifts to me. Your faith has strengthened mine, and you've ministered to me more than you'll ever know.

Dr. Rylander and Dr. Chen—My work and life mentors. I treated you both like fathers, who have supported me as I explore my purpose—whether in medicine or in personal reinvention. Your encouragement for my mission trips, both local and international, has been so valuable. Your generosity is a blessing I deeply appreciate.

My work family—Your kindness, encouragement, and daily example have inspired me to live out my faith with integrity and grace.

To my small group Bible study ladies—Cara, Jessica, Beth, Cherie, and Kathleen—I am grateful for each of you. We've walked through ups and downs together, and through it all, your fellowship and your hunger for the Lord have been such a blessing to me. "Iron sharpens iron" (Proverbs 27:17), and that is exactly what you have been in my life.

Thank you to those who read my work and offered feedback and encouragement: Jim, my love; Dr. Chen; Jody; Marilou; Cara; Ines; Hailey; Jen; and Kathleen.

TJ and Ines—Thank you for inspiring two of my chapter titles:
Chapter 21: Your Circle Matters

Chapter 22: Clean Me Up Inside (inspired by you, TJ).

Your influence has shaped these words more than you know.

Taneal Photography—Thank you for always capturing our vision so beautifully, whether it's individual moments or our whole family together. This moment is extra special, and you once again brought it to life with your incredible eye. We appreciate you more than you know.

To our five children, whose lives continue to inspire me in countless ways. And to my grandchildren, being your Lola fills my heart with pure delight.

My love, Jim—there will never be enough words to capture my gratitude for you. You have stood beside me through every season, cheering me on, lifting me, and supporting all of my "crazy" ideas with confidence that both humbles and inspires me. You are the quiet strength behind so many of my victories and the gentle comfort during the hardest moments, always believing in me even when I doubted myself. Your steady presence, your patience, and your unwavering faith in who I am have carried me through so many chapters of life. If there is someone I aspire to be like, it's you. You embody patience, generosity, and a love so genuine that it changes the people around you. You are love in action (1 Corinthians 13:4-8), and I am forever thankful to share this life with you."

Introduction:
I Wanna Be...

Second Corinthians 5:17 says...

> *"Therefore, if anyone is in Christ, he is a new creation: old things have passed away; behold, all things have become new."*

Weeks before I started writing, I had some moments when I would wake up around the same time every morning, around 3 AM. It must have happened three or four times. I would wake up, be wide awake, and just wonder what I was waking up for. I chose to go back to sleep. The third or fourth time, I began to wonder, *Oh my, is the Lord waking me up? If so, why?* Still, I did not get up; I chose to go back to sleep. I prayed while lying there, and it did not take long for me to fall back asleep.

"What is it, Lord? I don't know if it's just me or if You're really speaking." I did not hear it audibly, but it was an impression, perhaps? But I felt it gentle, yet firm: ***"Get up and write."***

Write? Me? No way. That has to be a dream. I have so many things I want to accomplish in life, places to go and see, but writing is definitely not on the list. Not even close. That's not me. I'm not a writer. Sure, I've kept journals on and off, but even that has been few and far between.

Maybe this is not about being a "writer." Maybe this is about obedience.

This reminded me of the story in 1 Samuel 3. It was the third time the Lord called, "Samuel!"

Samuel got up, went to Eli, and said, "Here I am. You called me."

But then Eli realized that the Lord was calling the boy, so he told Samuel, "Go and lie down, and if He calls you, say, 'Speak, Lord, for your servant is listening.'" So Samuel went and lay down in his place.

The Lord came and stood there, calling as at the other times, "Samuel! Samuel!"

Then Samuel said, "Speak, for your servant is listening" (vs. 8-10).

Now, I'm not Samuel, but because of that story, I got up. I asked the Lord, "What am I to write? I'm not a writer, but here I am, Lord, hesitantly surrendered." My heart's emphasis was on the word hesitant.

Moses expressed hesitation and offered several excuses when God called him to lead the Israelites out of Egypt (Exodus 3:11, 4:17). Specifically, Moses initially stated, "But I am not an eloquent speaker" and pleaded for God to send someone else (Exodus 4:10-13).

This is something I would not have imagined, especially when I began to hear God tell me to write about ***devotion!*** Now, I have really lost my mind.

Disclosures: I am not a theologian, nor have I gone to school with any Bible course. Religion was touched on during college as a minor subject. You can only imagine how seriously I took that subject. I used to open my Bible to whatever page and read what made sense for the day. I would usually say to myself, admiring others, "Wow, how I want to be like them. They can just blurt out the Bible verses just like that, word for word, with the address for reference!" I frequently render Scripture passages in paraphrase form. I read my Bible, but if I wanted a fast reference, I turned to Google to search for the Bible verse, then referred back to my Bible.

> *"Now to him who is able to do immeasurably more than all we ask or imagine, according to his power that is at work within us, to him be glory in the church and in Christ Jesus throughout all generations, for ever and ever! Amen." (Ephesians 3:20-21).*

When you've done what's familiar all your life and God calls you to visit a different direction, it feels like you're reinventing yourself. What do you do with that? So many questions fill your mind and heart. Am I hearing right?

Me? Confused? Absolutely!

A sense of uncertainty about the unknown and unfamiliar left me baffled whether the impression was from the Lord or simply an illusion of my own. Yet in the midst of it all, there became a burning desire to complete the task. A sense of excitement. A quiet thrill. I became very excited! I could not wait to keep writing. Soon, a sacred rush was felt from the inside out, deep down to my bones, heart, and overflowing to my skin. When it's God, your heart races, and uncertainty rises at the same time, and the goosebumps of what God has in store for you and others to experience. When it's God, you know it has to be ***great!***

He did not promise it would be easy:

> *"In this world you will have troubles, but take heart, I have overcome the world" (John 16:33).*

So, Lord, here I am. How can I serve? Hesitant. Humbled. Surrendered. And very excited.

"God doesn't call the qualified. He qualifies the called."[1]

I am praying and keeping in mind these words.

> *"Trust in the LORD with all your heart and lean not on your own understanding; in all your ways submit to him, and he will make your paths straight." (Proverbs 3:5-6).*

You drive, Lord, and I will follow the map.

> *"Come and follow me, I will make you fishers of men" (Matthew 4:19).*

> *"...Obey me and do everything I command you, and you will be my people, and I will be your God. (Jeremiah 11:4)*

Self-talk: Pour out your heart, but don't forget to focus on your source: "You are the Messiah, the son of the living God" (Matthew 16:13-20)

As you read through these pages, I want you to know that these are not my words. They didn't come from me. The Lord has given every word. Once I obeyed and accepted the task, I could barely type fast enough. Multiple Bible verses were compiled that I believe align with each message. I prayed I've done justice to what He has entrusted me with.

---

[1] Batterson, Mark. *The Circle Maker; Praying Circles around Your Biggest Dreams and Greatest Fears.* Grand Rapids, MI: Zondervan, 2011.

If only one person gets closer to God or one soul gets saved because of this book, then I consider that a considerable win.

I am humbled, honored, and completely fully aware that this is His work. I am grateful for the opportunity to be a part of it.

I've wanted to be many things in life. I am purely wanna be.

1
With God, All Is Possible

I've always enjoyed watching a kindergarten graduation. They would usually feature a slideshow of the kids, saying what they want to be when they grow up. Excited and unafraid.

Remember when anything was possible as a child? Wanting to be a doctor, a lawyer, a princess, and a mermaid all at the same time? How about a firefighter, a cop, a vet, and a superhero, too? A towel as a cape, using every piece of furniture as part of the adventure, and turning your backyard or street into the world of your imagination.

The places you visited in those childhood adventures—places far beyond what your eyes could see—were only limited by your imagination. Dinosaurs! You were leaping from rock to rock to escape the lava, followed by a massive boat with a river of chocolate and waterfalls made from your favorite drink (for me, it was Sunny Delight). And then, out of nowhere, the villain arrives. No matter how fierce the villain was or how intense the lava flowed, we didn't fear. We had superpowers, and we could face every challenge together.

In those adventures, there were no barriers to being who we wanted to be.

I remember those days—playing in the woods without a care in the world.

We'd come home just long enough for lunch, maybe a little siesta, then head right back out, making sure to return home before dark, or else you'd be facing a different adventure with your parents. We were everywhere—climbing trees, running, hiding, turning every corner into a new adventure. Life felt simple, wild, and full of wonder.

Once again, everything was always possible. No doubts, no anxieties, no "what ifs."

Reflecting as a Child

Grandma used to say, "Don't rush growing up; enjoy being a child."

Jesus teaches in Matthew 18:3-5.

> *"And he said, "Truly I tell you, unless you change and become like little children, you will never enter the kingdom of heaven. Therefore, whoever takes the lowly position of this child is the greatest in the kingdom of heaven. And whoever welcomes one such child in my name welcomes me." (Matthew 18:3-5).*

Psalms 116:6-7 reminds us.

> *"The LORD protects the unwary; when I was brought low, he saved me. Return to your rest, my soul, for the LORD has been good to you." (Psalms 116:6-7)*

In 1 Timothy 4:12, Paul encourages us, "Don't let anyone look down on you because you are young, but set an example for the believers in speech, and conduct, and love, and faith, and in purity."

In Matthew 19:14 and Luke 18:16, Jesus tells us, "Let the little children come to me, and do not hinder them, for to such belongs the kingdom of God."

As adults, we often think we know so much, having lived through so much, supposedly wiser. Yet when we pause to observe a child, we realize there's so much we can learn from them. And occasionally, we long to return to those simpler days, to live with the same carefree faith and wonder.

I wanna be rooted in childlike faith, so let's return to that childlike faith—rooted, unshakable, and full of possibilities.

Reflection

When we face the impossible, we must remember that we serve the God of the impossible. What looks like a dead end to us is just a new beginning in His hands. As we go forward, may we hold tight to the truth that nothing is too hard for Him. Dreams can rise, chains can break, and miracles can happen because with God, all things are possible.

Question

How can you embrace the simple, trusting faith of a child in your relationship with God today?

Gratitude

Thank you, Lord, for the gift of childlike faith, pure, trusting, and full of wonder. Help me hold onto that faith always, trusting You completely with an open and humble heart. Amen.

2
Memories

Have you ever met someone and listened to their memories from childhood?

A child who grew up too quickly? Who had no choice but to shoulder adult responsibilities? A child too young to be a provider for their family? Too young to lose loved ones? Too young to take the weight of survival? A child forced into resilience, not by choice, but necessity?

A child who felt abandoned…

Growing up with pain. Growing up with anger. Growing up with hurt. Growing up numb. Growing up with doubts. Growing up feeling alone. A child whose childhood was robbed, their innocence stolen, yet kept going. Through it all, they found forgiveness. They found healing. And somehow, through it all, they found love.

If they didn't have parents who tucked them in at night, who read them stories? Who kissed their boo-boos and wrapped bandages around their wounds? Who treated them to ice cream or simply held their hand? Who played with them? Who comforted them when they were scared or lonely?

There were times growing up I felt abandoned. But looking back now, I see the sacrifices that had to be made—for protection, for survival, and to get us to where we are today.

Over time, I've learned to piece together what once felt missing. And in doing so, the healing began. Understanding doesn't erase the pain, but it brings peace.

When you are in these situations or have been in these situations, be comforted, child, because God sees you.

> *"See what great love the Father has lavished on us, that we should be called children of God! And that is what we are! The reason the world does not know us is that it did not know him." (1 John 3:1).*

You are never alone.

God promises several times throughout the Bible to fear not.

> *"Have I not commanded you? Be strong and courageous. Do not be afraid; do not be discouraged, for the LORD your God will be with you wherever you go." (Joshua 1:9)*

> *"So do not fear, for I am with you; do not be dismayed, for I am your God. I will strengthen you and help you; I will uphold you with my righteous right hand." (Isaiah 41:10).*

It is so comforting that the Lord is always with me, I will not be shaken (Psalms 16:8). God is with you.

> *"The LORD your God is with you, the Mighty Warrior who saves. He will take great delight in you; in his love he will no longer rebuke you, but will rejoice over you with singing." (Zephaniah 3:17).*

God reminds us in John 14:15-21, ***"I will not leave you as orphans.*** I will come to you. The one who loves me will be loved by my Father, and I too will love them and show myself to them."

God has a purpose for you.

For we are God's handiwork, created in Christ Jesus to do good works, which God prepared in advance for us to do (Ephesians 2:10).

Just as our parents fell short, so do we in our own turn at parenthood. I'm sure there have been times when my kids have felt abandoned and maybe other times overwhelmed by my presence. Parenting is a delicate balance we're constantly trying to figure out. But what brings me comfort is this: our Father in heaven never misses the mark. He is always present, always faithful, and always enough, even when we are not.

I wanna be comforted with the comfort that only comes from the Lord's loving touch, loving guidance, and loving presence.

Reflection

Though we may grieve the simple joys we can no longer take back, we are not forsaken. The God who watched over our first steps does not abandon us in the wilderness of growing up. He redeems even the empty spaces. Childhood may be abandoned, but we are not. For in Him, every lost moment is remembered, every wound is seen, and every heart, no matter how grown, is still held in the arms of a Father who never lets go.

Questions

What "lost" moments from your past do you see God is gently redeeming or reminding you He has not forgotten?

How might trusting His presence in those empty spaces bring healing or renewed hope today?

Gratitude

Lord, I thank you for the simple joys of childhood—the laughter, the wonder, the small moments—that shaped my heart. Even for the things lost along the way, I do believe that none of these were wasted in Your hands. You have seen my tears, heard every unspoken word, and held every piece of my story with care. Thank you for being the God who redeems the empty spaces and turns them into sacred ground. In You, nothing is truly lost. Amen.

3
Peace

Yes, peace and quiet at last!

How many times have we whispered this sigh of relief?

Everyone's tucked in, the kitchen is clean, the laundry is folded, and work tasks are done. Maybe it's after a long day with the kids, a whirlwind at work, or an emotional stretch of weeks when life has felt all over the place. That quiet? It feels like a reward. But even that kind of peace is temporary.

What about a deeper peace? A peace that doesn't depend on finished tasks or silent rooms?

> *Jesus said, "Peace I leave with you, my peace I give you. I do not give to you as the world gives. Do not let your hearts be troubled and do not be afraid" (John 14:27).*

One night during dinner, my son—smart, curious, and always thinking—asked, "Why do we need Jesus?" But then he added, "Explain it without using the Bible."

We went back and forth. He had valid points I couldn't fully answer. I'm not always eloquent, and my words fell short. Finally, I looked at him and said, "I can't explain everything. But I've lived my life without Jesus, and I've lived with Him. And I would choose Jesus every time."

We looked at each other with quiet understanding. The conversation stayed with me. It made me reflect: What does peace really look like? And where do we find it?

Know Jesus, Know Peace.

No Jesus. No Peace.

Real peace isn't the absence of noise, but the presence of Jesus in the noise.

Peace is staying grounded in a storm, holding on to the promise of the one who calms it.

It was through knowing Jesus that I also learned to pray. And through prayer, I found peace.

Know Prayer, Know Peace.

No Prayer. No Peace.

Romans 8:26 reminds us of this.

> *"In the same way, the Spirit helps us in our weakness. We do not know what we ought to pray for, but the Spirit himself intercedes for us through wordless groans."*

Yes, I've had seasons like that. Too overwhelmed to form sentences. Too tired to begin. Praying with words that felt empty. But I kept praying. Why? Because Jesus told us this about prayer.

> *"Pray continually" (1 Thessalonians 5:17).*

> *"Devote yourselves to prayer, being watchful and thankful." (Colossians 4:2).*

And so I do. I pray when I'm worried about our kids. I pray when I wonder where they are in their walk with Jesus. Sporadically,

I panic, but my husband gently brings me back. "Remember your own journey at their age," he says. And I remember, God was patient with me. He's patient with them, too.

And in that remembering, peace returns.

> *"Do not be anxious about anything, but in every situation, by prayer and petition, with thanksgiving, present your requests to God. And the peace of God, which transcends all understanding, will guard your hearts and your minds in Christ Jesus." (Philippians 4:6-7).*
>
> *"The LORD gives strength to his people; the LORD blesses his people with peace." (Psalms 29:11).*
>
> *"I have told you these things, so that in me you may have peace. In this world you will have trouble. But take heart! I have overcome the world." (John 16:33).*

I want to be a master at holding on to peace, not the kind that fades, but the kind that anchors.

Because Jesus is the Prince of Peace.

He is the source of it.

And I know that God has a plan for me, for us, our kids, and the generations to come (Jeremiah 29:11).

Yes, prayers draw us closer to Jesus.

His Word is alive. His promises are still "yes" and "amen."

I wanna be a true prayer warrior. I wanna be always at peace. But more than that, I wanna be a child of a God who promises both.

Reflection

Peace is not found in the absence of problems, but in the presence of Christ. When prayer becomes a way of life, peace becomes our steady companion. Without prayers, we rely on our own strength and lose sight of God's power and promises. But when we know Jesus and seek Him daily, peace guards our hearts, even in uncertainty. Prayer connects us to the Prince of Peace, reminding us that we are never alone, never forgotten, and always held in His care.

Questions

In what way can you deepen your daily connection with Jesus through prayer so that His peace becomes your constant reality rather than a fleeting moment?

Are you longing for peace?

How can you turn your worry to worship today?

Gratitude

Lord, I am grateful that true peace is found in You alone. Thank you for the gift of prayer, where I can lay down every burden and receive Your perfect peace. I praise You that in knowing You, my heart finds rest, my mind finds clarity, and my soul finds strength. You are my peace in every season. Amen.

4
The Talk

When you hear, "Talk to your dad," or, "We'll have to talk to your dad," it usually signals something important. Maybe it's about making a big decision, something both parents need to weigh in on, or maybe you've done something that's earned "the talk."

Whatever the case, it often carries a sense of gravity. But it's not always a bad thing.

Sometimes, there's unique wisdom that fathers carry—different from the nurturing perspective of a mother. That balance, when healthy, brings strength and guidance.

When life gets overwhelming and uncertain, we often hear our brothers and sisters in Christ say, ***"Just talk to God."*** And sometimes, let's be honest, that seems a bit too simple.

Talk to God? The King of all Kings? The Maker of heaven and earth? The one that holds the universe in His hands? Just "talk" to God? Just like that?

> *"In him and through faith in him we may approach God with freedom and confidence." (Ephesians 3:12).*

Yes, just like that. Because He's your Father.

Some may have or have had a great relationship with their earthly father, but what about those who didn't?

I love watching my husband being a great dad and how he interacts with all of our kids. I'll focus on the girls for now (daughters and granddaughters are truly heartwarming). Taking them on lunch dates, helping them with projects, late-night calls, and just being an ear to listen and a shoulder to cry on is such a gift.

Hearing phrases like, "I just had a talk with her," "I just talked to Dad," or, "Papa talked to me."

These are all experiences I never had.

Seeing him dance and play with our granddaughters fills me with a deep sense of peace because they don't have that empty space to fill. Hearing my husband say, "I just talked to her," meaning our daughters or granddaughters, is music to my ears.

As I watch their joy, I can't help but imagine my younger self would be giggling with that same laughter, receiving the affection of a loving father. It's healing in a way—watching what love looks like through them.

One's perception of a father can affect how they view "the Father," yet simply coming to our Father in heaven and speaking your heart is considered prayer. We can talk to the Father whenever, wherever, all the time. What an inspiring truth that we can approach the Almighty God, and He hears us. He answers, knowing He is in full control and **working for our good**. Hard to fathom, but true.

We have a reminder from Matthew 11:28-30 that He always invites and always gives.

> *"Come to me, all you who are weary and burdened, and I will give you rest. Take my yoke upon you and learn from me, for I am gentle and*

> *humble in heart, and you will find rest for your souls. For my yoke is easy and my burden is light." (Matthew 11:28-30).*

The kids know, "Dad will answer, no matter what time and where." Just like the Father, always inviting.

> *"Call to me and I will answer you and tell you great and unsearchable things you do not know." (Jeremiah 33:3).*

Even if your earthly experience was the same as mine with a father who was distant, painful, or incomplete, I know God is not like that. I've experienced it.

I know He is near.

He is present.

He is listening.

He delights in hearing from me.

He delights in hearing from you.

I wanna be that daughter who is always talking to the Father.

Reflection

While our Father in heaven is sovereign and holy, He is also personal. He is our Father—intimately involved in every detail of our lives, inviting us to come freely, to speak openly, and to rest in His presence.

Talking to God doesn't require perfect words, long explanations, or polished presentations. It just requires a willing heart.

Question

When was the last time you "just talked" to God—not with fancy words, but with honesty and trust?

Gratitude

Thank you, Lord, for being a Father who listens, not because of who I am, but because of who You are. Thank you for giving me direct access to Your heart. I'm grateful that I don't have to perform or prove anything—I can just come. Help me trust You enough to talk to You more and find peace in Your presence. Amen.

5
Calling God in Troubled Times

When you only call God when you're in trouble, you're in trouble.

I read this, and boy, did I feel convicted. Have you ever treated the Lord as your 911 call?

Guilty as charged

Life is busy. Deadlines pile up, the kids need attention, and events fill the calendar. Add your side hustle, and work never stops. Somebody's got to do the laundry and cook the chicken, right?

It's an ongoing and revolving door of checklists.

Luke 10:38-40 tells the story:

> *As Jesus and his disciples were on their way, he came to a village where a woman named Martha opened her home to him. She had a sister called Mary, who sat at the Lord's feet listening to what he said. But Martha was* ***distracted*** *by all the preparations that had to be made. She came to him and asked, "Lord, don't you care that my sister has left me to do the work by myself? Tell her to help me!" (Luke 10:38-40).*

Martha wasn't doing anything wrong. She was ***serving Jesus***! She was taking care of important things. But in her busyness, she missed what mattered most: ***being with Jesus***.

How often do we do the same? How do we balance being Martha and being Mary?

> *He says, "Be still, and know that I am God; I will be exalted among the nations, I will be exalted in the earth." (Psalms 46:10).*

Be still. This is tough to do for the Marthas in the house (raising my hand in the background).

Running in circles. Exhausted. Drained. Caught in the never-ending to-do list of life, yet somehow feeling unproductive at the same time.

Jesus never said not to work. ***Even God is always at work***. But while we work, are we choosing what is better? Are we seeing Him in the busyness? Do we only call on God when we're in trouble?

> *"Look to the LORD and his strength; seek his face always." (Psalms 105:4).*

Not sometimes. Not just when life falls apart. ***Always***.

Let's be real—how often do we call on the Lord or pray only when we need something?

Do we only call when we're stuck in a situation we can't fix?

Do we only call when the bills are overdue?

Do we only call when the doctor's report isn't good?

Do we only call when we are at the end of our rope?

And then we cry out, "Lord, help me!"

Seek Him. Talk to Him. Walk with Him. Every day.

> *"Rejoice always, pray continually, give thanks in all circumstances; for this is God's will for you in Christ Jesus." (1 Thessalonians 5:16-18).*

Do me a favor, stop and reflect. What would you like in response when you call on the Lord?

> *"Call to me and I will answer you and tell you great and unsearchable things you do not know." (Jeremiah 33:3).*

> *"Remain in me, as I also remain in you. No branch can bear fruit by itself; it must remain in the vine. Neither can you bear fruit unless you remain in me." (John 15:4).*

Our Lord also said…

> *"If you remain in me and my words remain in you, ask whatever you wish, and it will be done for you." (John 15:7).*

Compare John 15:7 with Matthew 7:21-23.

> *"Not everyone who says to me, 'Lord, Lord,' will enter the kingdom of heaven, but only the one who does the will of my Father who is in heaven. Many will say to me on that day, 'Lord, Lord, did we not prophesy in your name and in your name drive out demons and in your name perform many miracles?' Then I will tell them plainly, **'I never knew you.** Away from me, you evildoers!" (Matthew 7:21-23).*

Your choice.

I wanna be one who has an open line with the Lord, known by God, who hears Him say, "Well done, good and faithful servant" (Matthew 25:23).

Reflection

A relationship with God is meant to be daily, not occasional. When we only run to Him in crisis, we miss the joy, strength, and wisdom that come from walking with Him every moment. God desires to guide us in the ordinary, not just rescue us in the urgent. A life built on constant, open communication with Him leads to peace before the storms, not just desperation in them. Trouble will come, but when we know His voice and presence daily, we stand strong, ready, and unshaken.

Questions

Is your relationship with God built on daily connection or only on moments of crisis?

What can you do to deepen your daily dependence on Him before trouble comes?

Gratitude

Lord, thank you that You are always near, not only in times of trouble, but in every ordinary moment. I am grateful that You long for daily fellowship with me, not just desperate cries for help. Thank you for being patient and faithful, even when I forget to seek You first. Today, I choose to draw near, to walk with You daily, and to know Your presence in every season. Amen.

6
Your Basic Identity: Your Name

Imagine the hours, days, and even months your parents may have spent picking a name suited for you long before you were born. Some parents picked the names of their children years and years before they were born or thought of—name choices that were influenced or inspired by family, friends, cultural roots, or even favorite book characters or films. Some names make us laugh. Some make us wonder, "How in the world did they come up with that?" Some names end up suiting a person's personality perfectly, while others seem hilariously off. There are even entire books filled with baby names and their meanings—names drawn from languages around the world, from history, or simply from imagination. If you're a parent, remember those days?

Then there is the other side of names—the ones we *did not* choose. The labels. The insults. The names that cut, instead. We've all heard them, maybe even believed them. Words spoken in anger, rejection, or ignorance. Name-calling that degrades and tears down, instead of building up. Name-calling that breaks, instead of lifting, that destroys and oftentimes isolates.

But God sees beyond every label the world has placed on you.

I remember those days when I was younger, when my abilities were questioned. People doubted whether I would even finish high school. When I did, they said I'd never make it through college. And when I proved that wrong, too, there was always another reason to look down on me.

At first, I carried that weight heavily in my heart—the weight of not feeling seen, not being valued—but as I got older, I began to see it differently. What once hurt me became fuel. I used it to push myself, to rise higher, to prove them wrong. It drove me, and in a way, it became a blessing.

But that drive also hardened me. I was achieving, but I was doing it with a heart guarded by pain and pride—until God's grace found me.

Now, I look back and realize that I didn't overcome it because of my own strength. I accomplished those things through Christ, who strengthened me (Philippians 4:13). It's no longer about proving others wrong; it's about living out the purpose God placed in me. Every step forward is a testimony of His grace, not my glory.

God knows you.

In Luke 12:7 and Matthew 10:30, Jesus says, "But even the very hairs of your head are all numbered. Fear not, therefore; you are of more value than many sparrows."

Remember, your *real* name is the name that Jesus picked for you.

Straight from Hosanna Wong's monologue "I Have a New Name."[2]

He calls me His friend.

> *"I no longer call you servants, because a servant does not know his master's business. Instead, I have called you friends, for everything that I learned from my Father I have made known to you." (John 15:15).*

---

[2] Wong, Hosanna. Spoken Word. 2017. https://www.hosannawong.com/spokenword

He calls me His chosen.

> *"For we know, brothers and sisters loved by God, that he has chosen you" (1 Thessalonians 1:4).*

He calls me His workmanship. He calls me His art. He calls me handmade. He calls me purposed and fashioned for good things.

> *"For we are God's handiwork, created in Christ Jesus to do good works, which God prepared in advance for us to do." (Ephesians 2:10).*

He calls my body a temple. He calls it the residence of the Holy Spirit.

> *"Do you not know that your bodies are temples of the Holy Spirit, who is in you, whom you have received from God? You are not your own" (1 Corinthians 6:19).*

He calls me His messenger to the world.

> *"But you will receive power when the Holy Spirit comes on you; and you will be my witnesses in Jerusalem, and in all Judea and Samaria, and to the ends of the earth." (Acts 1:8).*

He calls me His child.

> *"So in Christ Jesus you are all children of God through faith" (Galatians 3:26).*

He calls me greatly loved.

> *"But God demonstrates his own love for us in this: While we were still sinners, Christ died for us." (Romans 5:8).*

He calls me free, free indeed.

> *"So if the Son sets you free, you will be free indeed." (John 8:36).*

He calls me brand new.

> *"Therefore, if anyone is in Christ, the new creation has come: The old has gone, the new is here!" (2 Corinthians 5:17).*

It's amazing how different these names are from the names I'm used to listening to."

When I heard this message, all I could do was listen to it over and over to remind myself who I am with the Lord. How the Lord values me. It became my daily affirmation.

I am fearfully and wonderfully made.

> *"I praise you because I am fearfully and wonderfully made; your works are wonderful, I know that full well." (Psalms 139:14).*

I am precious, honored, and loved.

> *"Since you are precious and honored in my sight, and because I love you, I will give people in exchange for you, nations in exchange for your life." (Isaiah 43:4).*

Remember, when you hear different names from what the Lord has called you, then you are to take every thought captive to make it obedient to Christ.

> *"We demolish arguments and every pretension that sets itself up against the knowledge of God, and we take captive every thought to make it obedient to Christ." (2 Corinthians 10:5).*

God made you. He never makes mistakes.

You are known. You are deeply valued. And you are named by the one who formed you.

Your truest name—the one that matters most—is the name Jesus calls you. Not the one written on your birth certificate, not the one the world may have thrown at you in pain or mockery, but the name spoken in love by your Creator.

I wanna be called only by the name You give me, Lord.

Reflection

When the world tries to define us by our past, our failures, or our achievements, let us remember who we truly are: chosen, redeemed, and deeply loved. Our identity is not found in titles, opinions, or circumstances; it is rooted in Christ alone. May we walk boldly in that truth, knowing we are not who the world says we are. We are who He says we are.

Questions

What are the fun names or nicknames your parents, friends, or someone special called you?

Where have you allowed the world, or even your own thoughts, to define your worth or identity?

How can you intentionally embrace and live out the truth of who God says you are?

Gratitude

Lord, I thank You that my worth is not determined by my past, my failures, or the opinions of others. I am chosen, redeemed, and loved by You. Thank you for calling me Your own and for giving me an identity that cannot be shaken by the world. Help me to walk confidently in the truth of whom You say I am, trusting fully in Your grace and purpose for my life. Amen.

7
The Power of Touch

Whether you work in the medical field or not, you know there is a significant ***power of touch***.

I remember the first time I touched my kids after they were born. You forget all the process of pregnancy, whether it was an easy, breezy pregnancy or a challenging journey, not to mention the long waiting and the pain during labor and delivery. The ***first touch***, your baby's first little grasp of a tiny hand around your finger, and the first cuddle, having their head pressed on your chest. I still get teary-eyed with these memories. Your pain melts away.

Multiple studies have strongly suggested that touch is a significant, if not primary, human connection, improving physical and mental health. Touch is a tool of expression beyond words, a form of nonverbal communication. It can be calming in a stressful situation. Touch reduces or even heals symptoms like pain, fear, and anxiety. Touch has been an instrument in the healing process. Touch connects us. Eckstein, Markus, Ivan Mamaev, Beate Ditzen, and Uta Sailer. "Calming Effects of Touch in Human, Animal, and Robotic Interaction—Scientific State-of-the-Art and Technical Advances."[3]

One time, I saw a patient whose spouse passed away three years prior. She teared up while relaying that she still missed his touch and

---

[3] *Frontiers in Psychiatry* 11 (November 4, 2020): 555058. https://doi.org/10.3389/fpsyt.2020.555058.

hugs daily. It was something about the human touch, she said, so she gets a massage weekly. From time to time, I am led to pray with my patient as we are finishing our visit. It did not come easily. In fact, I resisted it for a while. I'm not your typical touchy-feely person, nor do I pray out loud. But the Holy Spirit gets His way. Like a toddler, I obeyed hesitantly, and in time, it got easier. While praying, a touch on their shoulder seemed to calm a despairing moment. Even for a moment, a sense of peace and hope can be seen. Praying that at this moment, God will touch them, and they will feel healing through His way.

I've made sure our home is filled with hugs and snuggles. Our kids, grandkids, and every generation that follows will never lack love—not in this lifetime. No matter how hard the day was, when you walk through that door and are met with open arms, the weight of the world melts away. All that stress and weariness gets replaced by something greater: love, comfort, and connection.

Because in a home where affection flows freely, healing happens without words. And that's the kind of legacy I want to leave.

The first study of the benefit of touch was mentioned back in 1922 by Hammett, and a study of the sensory nerve was done in 1994 by Andolfo. Ardiel, Evan L., and Catherine H. Rankin. "The Importance of Touch in Development."[4]

---

[4] *Paediatrics & Child Health* 15, no 3 (March 2010): 153-56.https://www.google.com/url?q=https://pmc.ncbi.nlm.nih.gov/articles/PMC2865952

Andolfo, Ilaria, Seth L. Alper, and Achille Iolascon. "Nobel Prize in Physiology or Medicine 2021, Receptors for Temperature and Touch: Implications for Hematology."[5]

But Jesus has been touching people for healing, for comfort, since over 2000 years ago.

In Luke 8:45, Jesus asked, "Who touched me?" Let's read about the healing power of a touch.

> *"Who touched me?" Jesus asked. When they all denied it, Peter said, "Master, the people are crowding and pressing against you." But Jesus said, "Someone touched me; I know that power has gone out from me." Then the woman, seeing that she could not go unnoticed, came trembling and fell at his feet. In the presence of all the people, she told why she had touched him and how she had been instantly healed. Then he said to her, "Daughter, your faith has healed you. Go in peace." (Luke 8:45-48).*

> *"They came to Bethsaida, and some people brought a blind man and begged Jesus to touch him. He took the blind man by the hand and led him outside the village. When he had spit on the man's eyes and put his hands on him, Jesus asked, "Do you see anything?" He looked up and said, "I see people; they look like trees walking around." Once more Jesus put his hands on the man's eyes. Then his eyes were opened, his sight was restored, and he saw everything clearly." (Mark 8:22-25).*

Jesus came and touched them.

> *"But Jesus came and touched them. "Get up," he said. "Don't be afraid." (Matthew 17:7).*

---

[5] *American Journal of Hematology*. 97, no. 2 (February 1, 2022):168-70. https://doi.org/10.1002/ajh.26407.

I wanna be touched by God.

> *"I have been crucified with Christ and I no longer live, but Christ lives in me. The life I now live in the body, I live by faith in the Son of God, who loved me and gave himself for me." (Galatians 2:20).*

Reflection

One touch from God can heal what years of striving could not. When we are touched by His presence, we are never the same. Fear gives way to peace, shame to grace, and weakness to strength. As we live at this moment, may we carry the mark of His touch in our hearts and reflect His love in our lives. Because once God has touched you, you don't just move forward; you rise transformed.

Questions

Where in your life do you need God's healing, strength, or transforming touch today?

How can you allow His presence to change not only your heart, but also the way you live and love others?

Gratitude

Lord, I am grateful for Your touch that changes everything. Thank you for meeting me where striving fails, for replacing my fear with peace, my shame with grace, and my weakness with Your strength. Because of You, I don't just go on; I rise renewed, restored, and transformed. May my life reflect the beauty of Your touch to a world that desperately needs You. Amen.

8
Just in Time

"Early is on time. On time is late," Vince Lombardi, former Green Bay Packers coach, stated.[6]

I like to be early, and, yes, I value being on time. But the reality? I tend to run late more often than I care to admit. One small delay snowballs into another, like a domino effect. At times, I've wondered if delay isn't always a failure, but perhaps a form of protection. Maybe even a divine pause. Perhaps better things are waiting just beyond the moment of thought missed.

Phrases like "last minute," "in the nick of time," and "saved by the bell" have danced through many chapters in my life. Whether it's caring for patients in an outpatient clinic or a hospital, I've witnessed God's grace show up in powerful ways just in time. Near missed deadlines, almost lost opportunities, narrowly caught flights, and the unexpected turnarounds that could only be explained by something—or someone—bigger.

Timing is everything.

> *"There is a time for everything, and a season for every activity under the heavens" (Ecclesiastes 3:1).*

Speaking of being on time, on one of our trips, my husband and I woke to a loud *ding* from the phone. Now, I *love* silence—no beeping

---

[6] Lombardi, Vince. "Quotes." *Vince Lombardi Official Site.* Accessed October 2, 2025. https://vincelombardi.com/quotes/

notifications, no buzzing, just pure stillness. My phone alarm is the *only* sound it's allowed to make. So when that chime rang out in the early hours, it jolted us awake—my heart pounding in my chest.

I grabbed the phone. A weather alert. Our flight had been canceled!

Panic set in.

Now, here's airport math that we all know: Leave three hours early, then rush into the airport only to sit around for over two hours for your flight to depart. Our situation, however, was an entirely different scenario. ***Every minute counted.***

The kicker? Our connecting flight—four hours away—was still scheduled to leave on time. And we had to be on it. Missing that flight would throw off the entire schedule for our mission trip.

With no time to waste, we sprang into action. Thankfully, our ride (thanks, Brienne!) —an absolute champ—agreed to drive us all the way, four hours across the state, totally changing plans at the last minute.

Because sometimes, the mission begins *before* you even arrive.

Have you ever felt that God is running late? That His answer is taking too long or maybe not coming at all?

I have felt that way, too. But then I remember:

> *"But do not forget this one thing, dear friends: With the Lord a day is like a thousand years, and a thousand years are like a day." (2 Peter 3:8).*

> *"For the revelation awaits an appointed time; it speaks of the end and will not prove false. Though it linger, wait for it; it will certainly come and will not delay." (Habakkuk 2:3).*

Life often feels like a race. Just like our rushing to the airport, we do live life in a rush. Even our prayers can come with urgency, expecting quick results, fast fixes. We've taken life in a microwave form. But in doing so, we risk missing the beauty and growth in the slow-cooked process of God's timing. The message in the journey.

We can plan and even do what we can to expedite the results we would hope for, but the truth remains:

> *"Many are the plans in a person's heart, but it is the LORD's purpose that prevails." (Proverbs 19:21).*

Maybe the delay you're facing isn't denial. Maybe it's not God forgetting, but God preparing. Maybe it's a pause filled with purpose.

> *"In their hearts humans plan their course, but the LORD establishes their steps." (Proverbs 16:9).*

I wanna be always on time for the Lord, aligning myself according to His purpose.

Reflection

God's timing may not always align with our expectations, but it is always perfect. While we wait, He is working, shaping our hearts, preparing our path, and aligning every detail for our good and His glory. Let us trust not just in what God will do, but when He chooses to do it. May we find peace in the pause, strength in the silence, and hope in the waiting, knowing that in His time, everything will be made beautiful.

Questions

Have you ever experienced God's grace show up "just in time"?

Could it be that the delays in your life are actually divine detours?

Gratitude

Lord, thank you for always showing up, even when I don't. Thank you for covering my late moments with Your timely grace. Help me walk in step with You, trusting that Your timing is always right. Amen.

9
Safe Travels

I was sitting in the airport, waiting for my delayed flight… for the third time. I looked around at all the people surrounding me, each one absorbed in their own world, heads bowed over their own devices. Some were laughing at conversations I couldn't hear, some were deeply engrossed in a book, and others simply looked worn out. Worn from what, I don't know—life, travel, or waiting?

As the hours passed, I reflected. If I could somehow reclaim all of this time lost to delays, I might have met everyone in my corner of the airport. I could have shared stories, exchanged laughs, and learned their reasons for travel. Some were likely headed for vacation, a honeymoon, or a mission trip. Others might be moving toward a new chapter in life… or a final goodbye. Perhaps someone was enroute to a funeral. Some might be retiring while others were rushing to see a sick loved one. Business or pleasure?

Different journeys. One destination—for now.

We would all board the same plane. We may talk. Or we may pass the flight in silence, eyes closed and headphones in. Regardless, we would all sit together, traveling in the same direction.

"Safe travels," people often say. It's more than a well-wish; it's a hope wrapped in faith.

It reminds me of the verse in Proverbs.

> *"Then you will go on your way in safety, and your foot will not stumble. When you lie down, you will not be afraid; when you lie down, your sleep will be sweet." (Proverbs 3:23-24).*

As boarding began, each section was called. Boarding passes at the ready. One last scan before we were seated. And I wondered if ***my boarding pass was my ticket to see Jesus... Am I prepared?***

Would the scanner recognize me as belonging to His kingdom? How much baggage did I bring? Was it packed with gifts and offerings of love, or weighted down by burdens I refused to surrender?

As we prepared to take off, the pilot spoke. We placed our trust in this stranger—someone we've never met—believing he would take us safely to our destination. We didn't know him, yet we trusted him with our lives.

> *"Then Jesus told him, "Because you have seen me, you have believed; blessed are those who have not seen and yet have believed." (John 20:29).*

Wherever I go, You are there. You are familiar with all my ways (Psalms 139:3-10).

> *"You discern my going out and my lying down; you are familiar with all my ways." (Psalms 139:3).*

Can we trust the one who holds the key to the true final destination? The way, the truth, and the life?

> *"Jesus answered, "I am the way and the truth and the life. No one comes to the Father except through me." (John 14:6).*

The plane landed. Relief flooded the cabin. Smiles spread. We arrived safely, but it left me asking, "Who is the pilot in your life?"

Jesus doesn't just offer safe travel; He offers eternal arrival. He doesn't promise no turbulence, but He promises His presence. And that changes everything.

So whether you're boarding, waiting, or already flying, I pray you're traveling with Jesus. Safe travels, friends.

Who are you trusting to get you to your final destination?

I wanna be traveling with Jesus.

Reflection

Life is full of delays, detours, and unexpected layovers, but even in the waiting, there's purpose. Every face we pass, every moment we sit still, every journey we take—God can use it to remind us of the greater destination we're all moving toward.

Questions

I ask again: Who is piloting your life?

Are you trusting in your own plans, your own timing, and your own direction? Or have you surrendered control to the one who already knows your landing spot?

Gratitude

Father God, thank you for safe travels. Thank you for small moments that carry big meaning. For the reminder that every journey can draw us closer to You. Amen.

10
Your Words

When do we need air to breathe? ***All the time.*** Humans need about 550 liters of oxygen per day to survive.[7]

When do we need water to survive? ***All the time.*** The human body consists of up to 60 percent water. Without it, we can only survive a few days.[8]

I was having my devotion before church and decided to focus on one to two verses. I even decided not just to read them but to memorize them by heart. It would be nice when I reach the point that I don't rephrase anymore, and I could say the verses word for word. I was inspired by the song lyrics I heard from Leanna Crawford's "Still Waters," based on Psalm 23. The message of the song talks about writing the scriptures on your heart for when you need them. Like your tools at home or work, it's available when you need it. It's better to have it when you need it, than need it and not have it. I highly recommend this song.

When do we need the Word of God? ***All the time***.

Just as air and water are essential for physical life, God's Word is essential for our ***spiritual life.*** John 1 reminds us of this truth.

---

[7] Hall, John E. *Guyton and Hall Textbook of Medical Physiology*. 14th ed. Philadelphia: Elsevier, 2021.

[8] Hall, John E. *Guyton and Hall Textbook of Medical Physiology*. 14th ed. Philadelphia: Elsevier, 2021.

"In the beginning was the Word, and the Word was with God, and the Word was God"(John 1:1).

"For the word of God is alive and active. Sharper than any double-edged sword, it penetrates even to dividing soul and spirit, joints and marrow; it judges the thoughts and attitudes of the heart" (Hebrews 4:12).

His words sustain me.

In one of his messages, Francis Chan told a story about a group of Chinese Christians who were put in jail because of their faith. They could not bring the Bible to prison, so they tore different pages of the Bible and shared them with each other. They used the Bible to sustain their strength and faith. It was their lifeline while being persecuted.[9]

Jesus answered, "It is written: Man shall not live on bread alone, but on every word that comes from the mouth of God" (Matthew 4:4).

"As the rain and the snow come down from heaven, and do not return to it without watering the earth and making it bud and flourish, so that it yields seed for the sower and bread for the eater, so is my word that goes out from my mouth: It will not return to me empty, but will accomplish what I desire and achieve the purpose for which I sent it" (Isaiah 55:10-11).

"Your word is a lamp for my feet, a light on my path" (Psalms 119:105).

God's Word guides us.

---

[9] Chan, Francis. "Pastor Francis Chan's Powerful Weekend in Prison | Testimony & Reflection." *YouTube Video,* 18;47. Published November 16, 2018. https://www.youtube.com/watch?v=655YogpBYqY

"Your word, LORD, is eternal; it stands firm in the heavens." (Psalms 119:89).

There was a time when I was not into the Word of God. As you may already know, the Bible once seemed like the most boring book to me, difficult to understand, disconnected from real life, and, honestly, irrelevant. I didn't see much value in today's life.

But everything changed when I began to experience the power of its words personally. Life hits in ways I didn't expect, and in those moments of struggle, confusion, and even joy, I started to see how the truths in Scripture were not just words on a page; they were alive and active. It was not an overnight thing; it was a process, a journey. Verses that once felt meaningless began to speak directly to my heart. I found comfort, guidance, conviction, and even purpose.

I remember seeing a billboard once while traveling that read: ***B.I.B.L.E.—Basic Instructions Before Leaving Earth***. At first, I smiled at the clever phrase. It was catchy, and it made you think. But the more I walked with God, the more I realized how true that message was. The Bible is not just a rule book or a history lesson; it's a ***survival guide***. It's my daily bread, my water, my air. Just as I need those things to live physically, I need His Word to live spiritually.

Now, I can't imagine life without it. What was once boring has become beautiful. What once felt irrelevant is now irreplaceable. God's Word was my anchor, my compass, and my lifeline.

"The grass withers and the flowers fall, but the word of our God endures forever." (Isaiah 40:8).

"Heaven and earth will pass away, but my words will never pass away." (Matthew 24:35).

> *"All Scripture is God-breathed and is useful for teaching, rebuking, correcting and training in righteousness, so that the servant of God may be thoroughly equipped for every good work." (2 Timothy 3:16-17).*

His Word is alive. It is life. It penetrates. It transforms.

I wanna be rooted in His Word.

Reflection

God's Word is not just ink on a page; it's life to our souls, light to our path, and truth in a world of noise. As we close this time, may we carry His Word in our hearts, letting it shape our thoughts, guide our choices, and strengthen our faith. The more we read it, the more it reads to us. So let us not only be hearers, but doers, living reflections of the Word that never fails.

Questions

How is God's Word challenging or shaping you right now?

In what ways can you live out His truth daily, so that your life reflects the hope and wisdom found in Scripture?

Gratitude

Lord, I thank You for the gift of Your Word, alive, powerful, and unchanging. Thank you that it speaks to my heart, reveals the truth in my confusion, and lights the way when the path is unclear. I am grateful that Your Word not only teaches, but transforms, shaping me into whom You've called me to be. Help me to not just hear Your Word, but to live it with courage and faith. Amen.

11
Go the Distance

I like jamming out to so many songs, regardless of what decade. Some songs just capture you, and you can't help but listen to them repeatedly. The same happens with praise songs: some feel as if God is speaking directly to you. They become prayers you whisper, praises you lift, and words you use to communicate your heart to the Lord at that moment.

That's exactly what happened to me the first time I heard "Go the Distance" from Disney's *Hercules*. Cheesy? Yes! But it is a powerful song. As I listened to it, it reminded me of some of the most powerful Bible verses. (Give the song a listen while you read the following verses).

Isn't it wonderful to know that when you arrive somewhere, a warm welcome is waiting for you?

> *"Then the King will say to those on his right, 'Come, you who are blessed by my Father; take your inheritance, the kingdom prepared for you since the creation of the world." (Matthew 25:34).*

> *"And you will receive a rich welcome into the eternal kingdom of our Lord and Savior Jesus Christ." (2 Peter 1:11).*

Sometimes, you just know in your heart you're where you're meant to be. It feels like home.

> *"And we know that all things work together for good to those who love God, to those who are called according to His purpose." (Romans 8:28).*

> *"For it is God who works in you to will and to act in order to fulfill his good purpose." (Philippians 2:13).*

> *"For I am not seeking the approval of people, but the approval of God, who judges my heart." (Galatians 1:10).*

In every trial, you push through because it is worth every step.

> *"I have fought the good fight, I have finished the race, I have kept the faith." (2 Timothy 4:7).*

> *"Fight the good fight of the faith. Take hold of the eternal life to which you were called when you made your good confession in the presence of many witnesses." (1 Timothy 6:12).*

It's a song about doing anything and going anywhere to find where one belongs. ***I belong to God because He calls us His children.***

The following verses express this promise:

> *"The Spirit you received does not make you slaves, so that you live in fear again; rather, the Spirit you received brought about your adoption to sonship. And by him we cry, "Abba, Father." The Spirit himself testifies with our spirit that we are God's children. Now if we are children, then we are heirs—heirs of God and co-heirs with Christ, if indeed we share in his sufferings in order that we may also share in his glory." (Romans 8:15-17).*

> *"If we live, we live for the Lord; and if we die, we die for the Lord. So, whether we live or die, we belong to the Lord." (Romans 14:8).*

> *"Because you are his sons, God sends the Spirit of his Son into your hearts, the Spirit cries out, 'Abba! Father!'" (Galatians 4:6).*

> *"See what great love the Father has lavished on us, that we should be called children of God! And that is what we are! The reason the world does not know us is that it did not know him." (1 John 3:1).*

> *"Before I formed you in the womb, I knew you, before you were born I set you apart; I appointed you as a prophet to the nations." (Jeremiah 1:5).*

We belong to each other. The children of God belong to his family forever.

> *"Now a slave has no permanent place in the family, but a son belongs to it forever"(John 8:35).*

We belong to a new identity in Christ.

> *"Consequently, you are no longer foreigners and strangers, but fellow citizens with God's people and also members of his household." (Ephesians 2:19).*

> *"But you are a chosen people, a royal priesthood, a holy nation, God's special possession, that you may declare the praises of him who called you out of darkness into his wonderful light." (1 Peter 2:9).*

This is a song of endurance and promise—trusting that we will get to where God wants us to be according to His purposes. Focus and hold on to God's promises.

It's a song of longing and looking for where we ***truly belong.***

All of us have our purpose. When found, we can go distances that we never imagined. Places you've been, people you've met, moments you've experienced, and lessons you've learned only because you are seeking His face.

Matthew 7:7-8 says, "Seek, and you will find." And in Luke 11:9–13, we see, "He who keeps on seeking finds."

By His grace, we stand firm and finish the journey.

> *"I can do all things through Christ who strengthens me." (Philippians 4:13)*

We can interpret the title alone as this: God went the distance to show His love for us. He sent His only Son as a sacrifice (John 3:16), who was nailed on the cross (Matthew 27:35; Mark 15:24; Luke 23:26; John 19:18, 23), and left the ninety-nine to find the one who wandered, and got lost (Matthew 18:12).

Let that sink in. Imagine leaving the ninety-nine just to come after me, the one who wandered. I mattered enough for Him to leave the ninety-nine just to save me. What was done for me, I can do the same. I enjoy even a fraction of leading one to Christ.

I wanna be going the distance to reach the unreachable to spread Your good news, Lord.

Reflection

God doesn't give up halfway; He goes the distance. He walks beside us when we're strong and carries us when we're weak. As we leave this moment, may we rest in the truth that the God who began a good work in us will be faithful to complete it. He's not done with you yet, and He never stops pursuing, never stops loving, and never stops showing up.

Questions

Where is God inviting you to go the distance, the extra mile, in your relationship, your work, or your service?

How can your willingness to go beyond what is expected reflect His love to others?

Gratitude

Lord, I am grateful that You went the ultimate extra mile for me, leaving heaven, walking this earth, and giving Your life so that I could live. Thank you for the strength to walk the second mile when the first feels hard enough. May my life reflect Your grace and generosity, not out of duty, but out of love for You. I praise You for every opportunity to serve more, love deeper, and give beyond what is required. Amen.

12
Warrior, Worrier

I'd like to think I am a warrior, but if I'm being honest, I probably walk more the road of a worrier. Most of the time, things I worry about are out of my control: our kids' future, their careers, who they'll marry, the grandkids, their careers, who they will marry, their walk with the Lord—the list just keeps piling up in my mind.

Yes, we are in a battle every day. Some days, we rise strong, like warriors. Other days, we're just trying to survive with the cloud of worry above us. But even in survival mode, there's grace, and God sees the warrior in us, even when all we see, is the weight of the worries we carry.

Being a ***warrior*** is no joke! If you look at history, known names and groups have been honored as the fiercest warriors, such as Alexander the Great, Joan of Arc, the Spartans, the Vikings, and many more. Even then, these warriors carried some worry in them.

David is considered a powerful, strong, aggressive leader and king in the Bible, yet you can feel his fear, worry, distress, and calls for help from the Lord. You can feel this in the book of Psalms, particularly chapters 18, 27, 42, 56, 62, 118, and 138. Despite all of these, he trusts in God.

Being a warrior doesn't always mean standing on a battlefield soaked in blood and fire. Sometimes, being a warrior means facing the relentless storms of life—the ones that come unexpectedly, without mercy.

It means holding your child in your arms as doctors diagnose lifelong conditions, and adjusting to new treatments, new fears, and new hopes as they grow. It's the heart of a mother breaking a thousand times, whispering desperate prayers in the dark, pleading with God to let her carry the pain instead.

And when you think it will never happen to you and your family, you hear your mother's doctor say, "Sorry, it's ***cancer.***"

My brain or heart? Fight or flight? Panic or pray?

I've never worn a military uniform. I've never held a weapon in war. I've only watched battles on screens and read about them in books.

But these moments—they feel like more than a war. They feel like standing in the eye of a hurricane with no shelter. Like lightning striking over and over (you know, those lightning strikes close to your home and the thunder shakes your house). Like a grenade going off inside your chest.

This is a different kind of war. Mom has been a warrior all her life. She's not loud, but her quietness reflects strength and control. She has faced so many storms and fought wars, wars that even for your worst enemy you would not pray for. This war is no different. She's facing this war in stride, and for that, you're a warrior, Mom. A hero I can look up to.

In the midst of all these, you can't help but be challenged in a spiritual battle. You can't question the Lord because He gives us this promise.

> *"I have told you these things, so that in me you may have peace. In this world you will have trouble. But take heart! I have overcome the world." (John 16:33).*

In the midst of all of these, I can't help but still boast in the Lord (Psalms 34:2). The news could have been worse. Did we worry? I would lie if we said no.

There is a comfort in knowing you're not the warrior, but God Himself will fight for you.

> *"The LORD will fight for you; you need only to be still." (Exodus 14:14).*

The only thing left to do, is to trust.

> *He says, "Be still, and know that I am God; I will be exalted among the nations, I will be exalted in the earth." (Psalms 46:10).*

I wanna be a warrior because with God, I can say, "Bring it on."

Reflection

There is peace in surrendering the battle to God. When we stop striving in our own strength and allow Him to fight for us, we discover a deeper kind of victory—one rooted not in control, but in trust. God does not call us to carry the weight alone, but to stand firm while He goes before us.

Question

Where in your life are you still trying to fight with your own strength instead of trusting God to lead the battle?

Gratitude

Lord, thank you for being with me when I am weak and when I feel defeated. I am grateful that I never have to fight alone. Amen.

13
The Armor

Nursing school felt like a boot camp—no joke. It was intense, demanding, and borderline military discipline. Before you could even set foot in the program, you had to pass through a gauntlet of requirements: entrance exams, interviews, and yes, a height qualification.

I still remember standing against the wall like a child, trying to get on a roller coaster ride, hoping I was tall enough to be allowed in. At four feet eleven inches, I knew I was probably going to miss the mark, but I stretched myself as tall as I could, trying to squeeze out just one more inch. The panel professors looked at me, then at the paperwork, then back at me. It was as if I wasn't even in the room as they spoke and deliberated.

Eventually, I was accepted—not for my height, but for academic performance. Thank God they let my brain do the talking! Now, I just had to keep my GPA up to par every semester, or I would get kicked out.

Once in, the roller coaster took off. Clinical days began with morning inspections—lined up like soldiers about to enter a battlefield. Our clinical instructor would check everything:

- *Uniform bright white, ironed with no wrinkles*
- *White shoes spotless*
- *Nails short, hair neatly tied up in a net, not a single strand on the collar*

- *Cap perfectly placed (yes, we still wore nurses' caps!).*

Then came the inspection of the clinical bag—a version of a soldier's gear. Stethoscope, working pens (various colors, of course), notepad, penlight, calculator, and medication book are ***all present and accounted for***. If something was missing, you didn't just get a warning; you risked being sent home.

After inspection, we gathered for prayer, and then we were off to what felt like the war zone of hospital floors. And as strict as it all seemed, I now realize ***we were being trained to be ready***. Prepared. Equipped. ***We were wearing our armor.***

Much like the armor Paul speaks of in Ephesians 6, we were not just going to a hospital; we were walking into people's battles—life, death, healing, grief—and we couldn't afford to show up unprepared.

What armor, weapons do you wear when dealing with the daily war of life? God has prepared us with the armor for eternity.

The Armor of God—Ephesians 6:10-18

In this powerful passage, God calls us to be strong in Him and in His mighty power. With His armor, we are equipped with spiritual armor, so that we can stand firm against every scheme of the enemy. The struggle is not always coming from our flesh, but from the darkness of this world, against spiritual forces. Stand firm. Stand our ground. Protected with the armor that will fight the battle with strife.

"Finally, be strong in the Lord and in his mighty power. Put on the full armor of God, so that you can take your stand against the devil's schemes." (Ephesians 6:10-11)

"And pray in the Spirit on all occasions with all kinds of prayers and requests. With this in mind, be alert and always keep on praying for all the Lord's people." (Ephesians 6:18)

The Pieces of Armor

- *Belt of Truth—buckles around the waist, so nothing can deceive your path*
- *Breastplate of Righteousness—protects the heart*
- *Shoes of Readiness—represents the gospel of peace*
- *Shield of Faith—extinguishes the flaming arrows of the Evil One*
- *Helmet of Salvation—protects the head*
- *Sword of the Spirit—the Word of God*

And we are to pray in the Spirit on all occasions, staying alert and always praying for all of God's people.

I wanna be wearing God's armor every day.

Reflection

There are days when we feel worn out, overwhelmed, or spiritually unarmed. But God never sends us into battle unequipped. He gives us His armor, not to hide behind, but to stand firm, to advance in faith, and to be victorious through Him. His strength becomes our strength. And when we clothe ourselves in truth, righteousness, faith, peace, salvation, and His Word, we are not just protected; we are empowered.

Questions

What's in your spiritual bag today?

Are you fully dressed in God's armor, or are there areas where you need to refocus and prepare?

Am I intentionally putting on the full armor of God each day, or am I stepping into battle unprepared?

Gratitude

Lord, thank you for not leaving me defenseless in a world full of battles. Thank you for every piece of armor You've provided, for the truth that guides, the faith that shields, the righteousness that protects, and Your Word that leads me forward. Help me to remember that the victory is already Yours, and I am simply called to stand firm in You. Amen.

14
Don't Quit

Family counseling can feel like a marathon. You start with hope, that "We got this!" attitude, ready to face the miles ahead, navigate every turn, and take on the ups and downs with steady strides. But somewhere along the way—through the long sessions, emotional setbacks, and silent car rides home—you wonder, is there any light at the end of the tunnel?

You ask, "Is this even working? Will we ever see change?"

The breakthroughs you hoped for seem delayed.

The process can be exhausting. Progress can feel painfully slow. You show up week after week. The breakthroughs are slow, and the silence in between can feel deafening. There are times you question if any of it matters—if healing is even possible. And the temptation to give up creeps in.

> *"Wait for the Lord; be strong and take heart and wait for the Lord" (Psalms 27:14).*

Yet, like a runner in the last stretch of a race, the key is to keep moving forward one step at a time. Even when you can't see the finish line, you trust it's there. Counseling, like healing, is not an instant sprint, but a patient journey. God is at work in the unseen moments, building endurance, compassion, and understanding in ways that will bear fruit in time.

> *"Blessed is the one who perseveres under trial because, having stood the test, that person will receive the crown of life that the Lord has promised to those who love him" (James 1:12).*

But then, something shifts. Weeks turn into months, and months turn into years.

And one day, you realize something has changed. Not just a little progress, but real, remarkable growth. Hope is no longer a distant idea; it's visible. Tangible. Alive in your home.

Keep going. Don't quit. Don't lose heart.

> *"Therefore we do not lose heart. Though outwardly we are wasting away, yet inwardly we are being renewed day by day. For our light and momentary troubles are achieving for us an eternal glory that far outweighs them all. So we fix our eyes not on what is seen, but on what is unseen, since what is seen is temporary, but what is unseen is eternal." (2 Corinthians 4:16-18).*

Healing may look different for each of us. But when you're in despair, give your focus to the Lord. Never quit looking up.

We may never fully understand the timing or the path, but know that God is in control.

> *"Trust in the LORD with all your heart and lean not on your own understanding; in all your ways submit to him, and he will make your paths straight." (Proverbs 3:5-6).*

If it seems slow in coming, wait. It's on its way. It will come right on time.

> *"For the revelation awaits an appointed time; it speaks of the end and will not prove false. Though it linger, wait for it; it will certainly come and will not delay." (Habakkuk 2:3).*

God's timing is perfect. He is never late or early. He knows the full story because He's the one writing it. And that story is always for His purpose.

I wanna be the one who perseveres, who never quits, and keeps trusting in His healing.

Reflection

Choosing not to quit doesn't mean the journey is easy; it means you're choosing faith over fear, hope over despair, and trust over control. You are walking in perseverance, and God honors that.

Questions

Where in your life are you tempted to give up right now?

What would it look like to trust God with that situation instead of quitting?

Gratitude

Lord, thank you for being faithful, even when I feel weary. Thank you for the strength to persevere, for the glimpses of healing, and for the reminder that You are never late. Help me to fix my eyes on what is unseen and to keep trusting and to never quit because You are not finished with my story yet. Amen.

15
Good Morning!

A gift of new beginnings. A new mercy.

The phrase "good morning" traces all the way back to the late fourteenth and early fifteenth centuries with roots in Old English and Germanic influence. It was used as a sincere wish for someone to have a good start to their day. Over the centuries, this simple greeting has carried a profound hope—that each new morning is a fresh start.[10]

I was never a morning person, but over time—whether you like it or not, especially when you start having kids—you're bound to wake up early. And somewhere along the way, I learned to embrace those early hours. Interestingly, when on vacation, waking up early is never a problem. I'm eager to explore new places, try local foods, and soak in the unfamiliar surroundings. There is something about morning energy—fresh and full of anticipation—that feels different.

Waking up with thankfulness and gladness has become a daily rhythm. It's not always easy, but each new day is a gift. Whether you're excited to start your morning routine—quiet time with the

---

[10] Oxford University Press. *"Good Morning, int. & n."* In *Oxford English Dictionary*. Accessed August 6, 2025. https://doi.org/10.1093/OED/3688942903

Origin and History of Good Morning. In *Etymonline*. Accessed August 6, 2025. https://www.etymonline.com/search?q=good+morning

Lord, a workout, or preparing for work—it's another chance. A new beginning.

> *"Because of the LORD's great love we are not consumed, for his* ***compassions*** *never fail. They are* ***new every morning;*** *great is your faithfulness." (Lamentations 3:22-23).*

> *"For his anger lasts only a moment, but his favor lasts a lifetime; weeping may stay for the night, but* ***rejoicing comes in the morning****." (Psalms 30:5).*

I've had my fair share of nights filled with weeping—over disappointments, fear, loss, or unknowns. But morning always brings a whisper of hope. A reminder that joy is still possible.

> *"Let the morning bring me word of your unfailing love, for I have put my trust in you. Show me the way I should go, for to you I entrust my life." (Psalms 143:8).*

There's something sacred about the early morning—before the noise, before the rush. You can lay your plans and your heart before God, offering the day to Him. You can start fresh, not because everything is perfect, but because He is faithful.

> *"In the morning, LORD, you hear my voice; in the morning I lay my requests before you and wait expectantly." (Psalms 5:3).*

I wanna be the carrier of joy in the morning and spread the hope to others.

Reflection

So when you say “good morning,” remember that it’s not just a greeting; it’s a declaration of gratitude. Of hope. Of faith in the one who gives us a new beginning every single day.

Questions

What does your morning look like lately?

Is it filled with routine or rushed moments?

Could it become a time of offering, of trust, of a new beginning?

Gratitude

Lord, thank you for mornings. For Your mercies that are new with every sunrise. Thank you for hope after weeping and the joy that rises with the light of day. Amen.

16
Grateful and Grumbling

How many times have you woken up thankful for the new day only to find yourself grumbling a few minutes later?

It's almost funny. One moment, you're whispering, "Thank you, Lord, for this morning," and then the next someone is saying, "You must have gotten up on the wrong side of the bed." The truth is, I can begin with a heart full of gratitude and still catch myself muttering under my breath about little inconveniences that test my patience.

Paul's words on this hit close to home.

"Do everything without grumbling or arguing," Philippians 2:14

It's humbling to realize that while I complain about small things, someone else is praying for what I take for granted:

- *The one in a wheelchair wishes to walk.*
- *The one walking wishes to run.*
- *The one on public transportation wishes for a car.*
- *The one who hates their job is being watched by someone who would take any job.*
- *The one unhappy with their house is envied by someone without one.*

I've been guilty of this thinking. It's not always greener on the other side. Sometimes, it's just different grass. Maybe you just need to water the grass.

There are times I focus too much on the outcome of my work, measuring my worth by my productivity and forgetting the Giver of my abilities. I push for more, add more to the checklist, and chase the satisfaction of accomplishment.

But the truth is, my life is already full. God has blessed me with things money cannot buy. Yet even in my abundance, I find myself ***grateful... and still grumbling***.

Paul's words in Romans echo my struggle.

> *"I do not understand what I do. For what I want to do I do not do, but what I hate I do. And if I do what I do not want to do, I agree that the law is good. As it is, it is no longer I myself who do it, but it is sin living in me." (Romans 7:15-17).*

> *"For I know that good itself does not dwell in me, that is, in my sinful nature. For I have the desire to do what is good, but I cannot carry it out. For I do not do the good I want to do, but the evil I do not want to do—this I keep on doing. Now if I do what I do not want to do, it is no longer I who do it, but it is sin living in me that does it." (Romans 7:18-20).*

> *"Thanks be to God, who delivers me through Jesus Christ our Lord! So then, I myself in my mind am a slave to God's law, but in my sinful nature a slave to the law of sin." Romans (7:25).*

There is nothing wrong with growing, improving, and striving, unless I lose sight of the ***main thing***. My main thing must always be Jesus.

So, I pause. I realign my heart with His purpose, not mine. I remind myself, He is enough.

> *"And in Christ you have been brought to fullness. He is the head over every power and authority." (Colossians 2:10)*
>
> *But he said to me, "My grace is sufficient for you, for my power is made perfect in weakness. Therefore I will boast all the more gladly about my weaknesses, so that Christ's power may rest on me." (2 Corinthians 12:9).*

We are enough.

> *"For we are God's handiwork, created in Christ Jesus to do good works, which God prepared in advance for us to do." (Ephesians 2:10).*

He provides.

> ***"Look at the birds of the air; they do not sow or reap or store away in barns, and yet your heavenly Father feeds them. Are you not much more valuable than they?" Matthew 6:26***

I wanna be aligned in gratefulness.

Reflection

Gratitude and grumbling can't really share the same heart for long—one will eventually push the other out. When we let gratitude lead, it shifts our perspective. The day may still hold challenges, but our spirit stays lighter. When gratitude fades into grumbling, it's a sign that my eyes have drifted from the Giver of the gifts. When we choose gratitude over complaint, we not only honor God; we make room for joy.

Question

What blessings am I overlooking because I'm focused on what I don't have?

Gratitude

Lord, thank you for the countless ways You have provided for me. Forgive me when I let discontentment steal my joy. Help me to see each day as a gift and to keep my heart fixed on You, the source of every good thing. Amen.

17
Who Wants to Be Second?

In the hustle and bustle of life, let's be honest… who wants to be ***second?***

We strive for first place in everything.

- *First place in sports.*
- *First place in school.*
- *First place at work.*

There's something about winning, standing on top of the podium, knowing you gave your best, and excelling to accomplish being on top. Even being ***first in line*** for a store sale or an after-Christmas bargain hunt feels like an accomplishment. We convince ourselves that if we don't make it to the store within minutes of it opening, the best deals will disappear, so we rush, strive, and push to be first. Best bargain for the materials just to shove them in our closet and forget later where we stored the stuff in times of need.

Some people want to be first on the latest and finest things. There is nothing wrong with wanting to be first, right? And why not? First place feels different. It carries a sense of pride and success. Even boarding a plane gives you a sense of getting seated first. Firstborn privileges. First rank. We chase ***"first"*** like it's the only position worth having. ***First. First. First.***

On the other side of the world, certain places have certain schedules. It is important to be first. Growing up, the water supply was limited at times. To be fair to all, they would open the community water supply (hand pump), either in the early morning or early afternoon, for a limited time. People will try to get in line early and ***be first***, so they can get the water they need. Even if you're in line, if the water supply runs dry, you're out of luck. Perspective of needing and of what being first in line means.

But then there's ***second place***.

Second place in a race—so close, but still not first. Second choice—the backup, the runner-up, the "if no one else is available." We even hear the phrase, "Second place is just the first loser."

It stings, doesn't it? Losing by a fraction of a second. Being the second choice for a job.

Feeling like you're the afterthought, the plan B.

But what if I told you ***being second isn't so bad***? If truth be told, ***being second is exactly where we should be***.

How about ***second chances***?

Second chances don't always come wrapped the way we expect. Sometimes, they come after resistance. After wrestling with God. After almost pushing away the very thing that might just be a fantasy, or maybe we're too afraid to pray for.

Allow me to explain.

When I met my husband—my love, my best friend—I was on an entirely different journey.

I was falling in love... with Jesus. I had entered a sacred space where I was learning intimacy with Christ. He was filling every empty part of me. I was discovering the meaning of agape love—that selfless, unconditional kind of love. The highest form of love. The kind that changes everything. And the beneficiary was me.

So, I was determined to protect it.

I didn't want anything—especially my flesh—to get in the way. I didn't want a relationship to distract me from what God was doing.

So, what did I do? I challenged God.

Have you seen the movie *How to Lose a Guy in 10 Days?* Yeah… I kind of did that. And more.

I got busy. I wasn't sure if I was praying or daring the Lord. "Lord, if this is really from You, then no matter what I do, even if I sabotage it, it will still happen."

And you know what? God, in His mercy, in His perfect love for me, showed me through my husband. He gave me a second chance. And He knew He had to show it in a tangible way.

He brought my husband and more (stepchildren and grandkids). Stepchildren who treated my kids like their own siblings.

The best bonus: a family

He sent me a God-fearing man. A man who loves the Lord more than he loves me, and for that reason, he loves me the way only God could provide. We are often asked how we met. If we could write it all or show it in a movie, it would be under the romantic comedy section. God has a great sense of humor.

Matthew 19:30 and 20:16 mention, ***"The first will be last and the last will be first."***

There is a group that focuses on being second called I Am Second. It is a non-profit organization and a United States multimedia movement designed to inspire people to ***"put Jesus Christ first."*** Its main goal encourages and introduces the idea of people restructuring their lives in a way that focuses on putting God first and self second. On their website[11] you will see multiple shared testimonies from all walks of life reveal the changes in their lives once they let God lead. We admit a living proof when we step aside and allow God to take the wheel. Jesus, first, always.

I ran into this accidentally while searching for something on YouTube, and countless story after story about how putting Christ first became the goal rather than their own. This helped me to focus on what matters most.

> *"But seek first his kingdom and his righteousness, and all these things will be given to you as well." (Matthew 6:33).*

To be able to be more, He must increase; I must decrease (John 3:30) because I know that God's grace is sufficient for me. After all, His power is made perfect in weakness. "Therefore, I will boast all the more gladly about my weakness, so that Christ's power may rest in me. That is why, for Christ's sake, I delight in weaknesses, in insults, in hardships, in persecutions, and in difficulties. For when I am weak, then I am strong" (2 Corinthians 12:9-11).

> *"For I am not ashamed of the gospel, because it is the power of God that brings salvation to everyone who believes: first to the Jew, then to the Gentile." (Romans 1:16).*
>
> *Jesus replied, "Love the Lord your God with all your heart and with all your soul and with all your mind. This is the first and greatest*

[11] https://www.iamsecond.com/

commandment. And the second is like it: 'Love your neighbor as yourself. All the Law and the Prophets hang on these two commandments." (Matthew 22:37-40).

Love God. This is the great and ***first commandment***.

"As for me and my household, we will serve the Lord," Joshua 24:15, because Jesus has conquered the world, John 16:25-33. It's not losing; it's winning. He is always leading, always guiding, always within reach.

Second is not so bad at all.

He is the foundation of all.

"For no one can lay any foundation other than the one already laid, which is Jesus Christ." (1 Corinthians 3:11).

True purpose and peace come when we stop striving for first place in our own lives and start putting God at the center.

When God is first, everything else falls into place.

I wanna be second because Jesus is first.

Reflection

When we choose to be second, it's not a sign of weakness; it's a declaration of faith. It means we've come to understand that life isn't about striving for the spotlight, but about surrendering to the one who already holds it. Letting God be first in our thoughts, decisions, and desires reorders our priorities and brings clarity to our purpose. Real purpose begins when we let Him take the lead.

Questions

In what areas of your life are you tempted to take control or be "first"?

How can you intentionally step back and let God lead, trusting His perfect will above your own?

Gratitude

Lord, I thank You that I don't have to strive for first place, for You are already there, sovereign, good, and faithful. I am grateful that being second in Your plan means I am fully known, fully loved, and perfectly cared for. Thank you for leading the way, for going before me, and for working all things for good as I choose to follow You above all else. Amen.

18
Count On It

When I gave my life to Jesus, I was all in—went in the boat of salvation, no brakes. I was in love. I was like a kid who ate a lot of sugar and was all over the place. I was on fire! Every conversation somehow turned into a testimony. I was that person. "Jesus this, Jesus that." If I had met you back then, I probably would have asked you which church you attended or would've invited you to church within five minutes of talking.

I went from thinking the Bible is the most boring book ever to not stopping to read it and wanting to know more about it. I was hungry and thirsty for the Word. My Bible that was given to me by my Bible study group is now falling apart, so I finally had to get another one. I still have that Bible, though. Every time I see that book, it reminds me of how God has carried me through some tough challenges.

I truly believed that after surrendering my life to Christ, it meant life would become easier, my struggles would fade, and pain would be a thing of the past. After all, if I was now walking with God, surely everything would just be easier. No more tears, and everything is in place, right?

Wrong.

Then came another storm. Another hardship. Another disappointment.

And I found myself asking, ***"Wait... wasn't this supposed to be different?"***

But then, John 16:33 reminded me, "I have told you these things, so that in me you may have peace. In this world, you will have troubles (Say what?). (Come again?). ***But*** take heart! I have conquered the world." Whew!

Thank goodness for the big ***"but"*** in that verse!

Yes, the storms will surely come, ***but*** remember in Mark 4, Jesus calms the storm.

Jesus has already won. He has already overcome.

We can count on the fact that trouble will come our way, but we can also count on something far greater:

Count on the Crisis

It's not a matter of if, but when. Hard times are inevitable. Even Jesus—God in the flesh—faced suffering, betrayal, and the weight of the world's sin. Why should our lives be any different? We will experience difficulties, but they are not the end of our story.

> *"I consider that our present sufferings are not worth comparing with the glory that will be revealed in us." (Romans 8:18).*

The pain is temporary. The glory is eternal.

Count on the Gospel

The good news of Jesus Christ is our anchor. When storms come, when questions arise, when life feels unfair, ***the gospel stands firm.*** It is not just a feel-good message on Sundays; it is ***the power of salvation*** and the ultimate hope we cling to every single day.

Philippians 1:6 gives us confidence.

> *"Being confident of this, that he who began a good work in you will carry it on to completion until the day of Christ Jesus." (Philippians 1:6).*

He isn't done with you yet.

Count on Christ

Above all, we can count on Jesus. Not on our strength. Not on the circumstances. Not on people. But on Him.

> *"The LORD your God is with you, the Mighty Warrior who saves. He will take great delight in you; in his love he will no longer rebuke you, but will rejoice over you with singing." (Zephaniah 3:17).*

No matter what we face. He is in control. And no matter how messy life gets. ***He is working all things for good.***

> *"The LORD will vindicate me; your love, LORD, endures forever—do not abandon the works of your hands." (Psalms 138:8).*

So when the storms come—and they will—count ***on it***, but also count on the one who walks on water in the midst of them.

He's got you.

I wanna be counting. Counting on the crisis. Counting on the words. Counting on Christ.

Reflection:

Life changes, people disappoint, and plans shift—but God remains steady. In every season, Christ is our solid rock and faithful provider. Trust His promises, lean on His strength, and rest in His unchanging truth. He is always enough.

Questions

What area of your life are you being invited to trust Christ more deeply?

How can you remind yourself daily to count on His strength instead of your own?

Gratitude

Lord, I thank You that I can count on You when everything else feels unsure. You are my anchor in the storm, my guide in the unknown, and my refuge in weakness. I am grateful that You never fail, never leave, and never change. Teach me to trust You more, to lean not on my own understanding, but to rest in Your perfect and unfailing care. Amen.

19
Go the Extra Mile

Have you heard the phrase "go the extra mile"? It sounds noble, even inspiring, but living it out is a whole different story.

When my husband and I were training for the Tough Mudder obstacle race, it wasn't just about strength or endurance, but mindset. Our training included plenty of running: short, long, and everything in between. There were days we ran three to five miles, then seven to eight miles, and sometimes even stretched it to ten miles. But here's the kicker—just when I thought I had hit that final mile and was ready to pour out everything I had left, my husband would say, "Don't sprint yet. There's an extra mile."

Ugh… not what I wanted to hear. That extra mile felt like the hardest part, not because of the distance, but because it asked something more of me when I thought I had nothing left.

It reminded me of the mission trips we took to China and Oaxaca, Mexico. I remember traveling to the mountains with all of our supplies, setting up a makeshift clinic, and before we knew it, people were lined up, many having walked miles just to be seen.

Some cases were simple, others heartbreaking and beyond what we could treat. But we offered the best healing we had: ***prayer***.

Time was tight. Darkness made the roads dangerous, and warnings came, yet we always said, "One more person… Just one more." We served until the very last moment.

That's exactly what Jesus teaches us in Matthew 5:41

> *"If anyone forces you to go one mile, go with them two miles." Matthew 5:41*

In the culture of that time, Roman soldiers could legally force civilians to carry their gear for a mile. Jesus wasn't just talking about physical endurance; He was calling us to a ***radical kind of love***, one that goes beyond what's expected, beyond what's comfortable. It's the kind of love that chooses the second mile, even when the first one wasn't fair.

This theme shows up again and again in scriptures:

> *"If someone slaps you on one cheek, turn to them the other also. If someone takes your coat, do not withhold your shirt from them." (Luke 6:29).*

> *"Let us not become weary in doing good, for at the proper time we will reap a harvest if we do not give up." (Galatians 6:9).*

> *"You have heard that it was said, 'Love your neighbor and hate your enemy.' But I tell you, love your enemies and pray for those who persecute you" (Matthew 5:43-44).*

These verses challenge us. They call us to dig deep, not just into our energy, but into grace, patience, and humility. That "extra mile" often looks like forgiving again, helping someone who won't thank you, or praying for someone who hurt you. It's not easy. It can feel just like that surprise mile at the end of a long run: unwelcome, exhausting, but transformative.

The extra mile is where character is refined, faith is tested, and love is proven. It's where we stop living for ourselves and start reflecting the heart of Jesus.

So the next time you're tired, frustrated, or feel like you've done enough, remember that might just be where the real journey begins. And trust me, God walks every step of that extra mile with you.

I wanna be extra trusting in the grace of the Lord. Extra on extending grace, patience, and serving others as if serving the Lord.

Reflection

Going the extra mile isn't about being seen; it's about serving like Jesus. It's in that extra step, that quiet sacrifice, where love shines brighter. When we give more than expected, we reflect the heart of God.

Question

When was the last time you went beyond what was expected to show love or serve someone, and how did it reflect Christ in you?

Gratitude

Lord, thank you for the strength to serve beyond what's comfortable. Thank you for showing me, through Jesus, what it means to love without limits. Help me walk the extra mile with joy, knowing it brings glory to You. Amen.

20
Bring the Light, Be the Light

Our love for adventures has built our traveling map, each place a mark of memory. One of the unforgettable places we visited was Mammoth Cave in Kentucky. Known as the world's longest known cave system, with more than 400 miles explored, it's also one of the oldest tourist attractions in North America.[12]

Touring this cave was a mix of history and thrill. There were narrow climbs, massive chambers, and dim paths, barely lit by soft guide lights. While there were lights installed along the way, they were intentionally faint, meant to preserve the cave's natural darkness and amplify its grandeur. Our tour guide carried a brighter light, which we used to illuminate areas we could barely see. Without being told, everyone naturally stayed close to the guide. You could sense the quiet trust—we needed his light to move forward.

What amazed me most was how quickly our eyes adjusted to the dark and, just as quickly, how they hurt when exposed again to sunlight. Darkness can be familiar, even comfortable. But when we're reintroduced to the light, it wakes something in us.

> *"God saw that the light was good, and he separated the light from the darkness." (Genesis 1:4).*

---

[12] Mammoth Cave National Park. "*Mammoth Cave.*" National Park Service. Last modified June 10, 2024. https://www.nps.gov/articles/mammothcave.htm

Isn't it amazing how Jesus always brings the light? Like that guide, He illuminates the way, and we follow. He is the light overcoming darkness, (John 1:5). When we walk with Him, we no longer walk blind. We become bearers of His light.

> *Jesus answered, "I am the way and the truth and the life. No one comes to the Father except through me." (John 14:6).*
>
> *"You are the light of the world. A town built on a hill cannot be hidden. Neither do people light a lamp and put it under a bowl. Instead they put it on its stand, and it gives light to everyone in the house. In the same way, let your light shine before others, that they may see your good deeds and glorify your Father in heaven." (Matthew 5:14-16).*

Let us be the light wherever we are.

I remember Hailey once joking, "Wherever you go next, I'm coming!" She had no idea what that would mean. A few weeks later, I invited her on my next trip. She was excited and curious to know where. A mission trip to Guatemala. Her face said it all. Where? What is a mission trip? She wasn't a believer. In fact, she'd once told me she wasn't into the "God thing." Still, after a few weeks, she came back to me and said, "Since I said I'd go anywhere, I'm going."

I gently reminded her that this trip was all about Jesus—day and night. She hesitated, but kept her word. During the trip, she showed up to serve: helping build a church, assisting in the clinic, playing with the children, and doing whatever was needed. She was ready to lend a hand. She didn't participate in prayers, but she was never dismissive, either. She sat there and stayed quiet, respectfully observing.

On our last day, we visited a small village with the local pastor. We went door to door, greeting and praying with people. At one house, an elderly woman greeted us with such joyful tears. Through translation—her native dialect to Spanish, then to English—she shared her dream.

She had seen travelers coming to her home to pray. In her dream, two people would come to know and give their lives to Christ: one from her village and one from far away.

As we ***gathered in a circle to pray***, Hailey sat quietly by the door. Others gently encouraged her to join. After some hesitation, she ***stepped into the circle***.

As we prayed, a strong wind suddenly rushed through. It felt powerful, almost storm-like. Our prayers grew louder, more heartfelt. When we opened our eyes, the wind calmed. Hailey was in tears. So was a young girl from the village.

That day, both gave their lives to Jesus.

Her life has never been the same. That was July 2018. Since then, she's led a youth group, organized prayer meetings, ***traveled*** with the youth camp, and continues to serve others with joy and purpose.

I once told her, "One day, you'll share your before-Jesus story and all He's done through your trials. Because even when you didn't know it, He was always there." As a light was shown to me once, so our purpose is to keep giving light to others.

Hailey, your story is beautiful. You're a living testimony of strength, perseverance, and grace. I'm so proud of whom you've become. Keep going. Keep surrendering it all to Jesus. As you share Him with others, you carry His light. Listen to the words of Jesus to the people.

When Jesus spoke again to the people, he said, "I am the light of the world. Whoever follows me will never walk in darkness, but will have the light of life." (John 8:12).

"You are the light of the world. A town built on a hill cannot be hidden. Neither do people light a lamp and put it under a bowl. Instead they put it on its stand, and it gives light to everyone in the house. In the same way, let your light shine before others, that they may see your good deeds and glorify your Father in heaven." (Matthew 5:14-16).

I wanna be the light that gives life.

Reflection

Being a light doesn't always mean preaching or knowing all the answers—it simply means showing up with love, kindness, and compassion. Just as Hailey once sat in quiet observation, many people in our lives may be watching how we live more than what we say. Our everyday choices—how we serve, forgive, encourage, and love—can point others to Jesus without a single word. Sometimes, being a light is just being present. Jesus said, "You are the light of the world. A city set on a hill cannot be hidden" (Matthew 5:14). When we walk with Him, we reflect His light. Let us not underestimate the quiet power of our testimony.

Question

How can you be a source of light today in your home, workplace, or community?

Gratitude

Lord, thank you for calling us to be light in a world that so often feels dark and uncertain. Thank you for trusting us to carry Your presence through our actions, words, and lives. Help us to shine brightly, not for our glory, but for Yours. Remind us daily that we are never alone in this calling. May others see You through us. Amen.

21
Your Circle Matters

"As iron sharpens iron, so one person sharpens another." (Proverbs 27:17).

Through the years, we have probably been in so many circles of people. The group of friends we played with at school and outside of school, growing up with kids in the neighborhood. Soon, everybody parted ways, either moving to a different home location or a different school, and with every chapter, we learned to be in another circle. Some circles are still alive. If you stayed in the same area, definitely the people you played with in your neighborhood are somehow still your friends.

One of the circles I have been honored to be a part of is my college classmates. What began as strangers turned into seatmates, groupmates, friends, and eventually, family. Over thirty years of friendship have been built through random class shuffles, nun-patrolled hallways (yes, it's tight attending a Catholic school), and shared memories of professors who pushed us hard.

Though we're now scattered across the globe, every reunion feels like no time has passed. From laughs to life talks, we continue to show up for each other, then and now. A true bond for life.

Then you also build relationships with your other circles, whether it's a work or business circle, a Bible study circle, an exercise circle, a book club circle, or whatever circle there is. The bond that develops, grows stronger and stronger as the years go by.

A simple invitation to attend a Bible study (thanks, Jen!). Thank you for inviting me, accepting me, and showing the love of Jesus from where I am at. A simple yes and the rest is history. This simple invitation started my intimate relationship with Christ. We have since formed and been in different Bible study circles, yet we have this bond that will forever be superglued strong.

> *"Accept one another, then, just as Christ accepted you, in order to bring praise to God." (Romans 15:7).*

Our sister and brother in Christ circle. A circle that is ***inclusive to all.*** A circle that encourages you to love your neighbor as yourself. "A new command I give you: Love one another. As I have loved you, so you must love one another.

> *"A new command I give you: Love one another. As I have loved you, so you must love one another. By this everyone will know that you are my disciples, if you love one another." (John 13:34-35).*

Because of our relationship with Christ, we are ***set apart.***

> *"For you are a people holy to the LORD your God. Out of all the peoples on the face of the earth, the LORD has chosen you to be his treasured possession." (Deuteronomy 14:2).*

For the circle that may not know Christ yet, make space and bring them to the circle.

> *"But in your hearts revere Christ as Lord. Always be prepared to give an answer to everyone who asks you to give the reason for the hope that you have. But do this with gentleness and respect, keeping a clear conscience, so that those who speak maliciously against your good behavior in Christ may be ashamed of their slander. For it is better, if it*

is God's will, to suffer for doing good than for doing evil." (1 Peter 3:15-17).

Following Christ doesn't come easy. Following the circle that follows Christ is even trickier because no matter what, we all fall short and still sin.

"For all have sinned and fall short of the glory of God, and all are justified freely by his grace through the redemption that came by Christ Jesus." (Romans 3:23-24).

I wanna be in the circle that Jesus leads.

Reflection

Being in the circle with Jesus means staying closer to His heart, walking in His truth, and living in His love. The closer we are to Him, the more we become like Him. Stay in His presence because there's no better place to be.

Questions

Are you walking closely with Jesus or standing on the outside looking in?

What's holding you back from stepping fully into His presence?

Gratitude

Lord, thank you for calling me close, inviting me into Your inner circle, where love, peace, and purpose are found. I'm grateful for Your constant presence, Your open arms, and the peace that comes from walking with You daily. You always make room for me, regardless of where I've been. There's no place I'd rather be than near to You. Amen.

22
Clean Me Up Inside

From time to time, my husband and I would participate in some adventures. One of those is the mud races, like Tough Mudder and Savage Race, to name a couple. These races consisted of over thirty obstacle races, climbing, crawling, running, swimming, carrying a log, turning wheels—you get the picture. You could only imagine what we look like after each race: sweaty, dirty, and yes, muddy.

We have also done a lot of mountain climbing, and at times, we would get to some areas where we would get really dirty. At the end of each race, they would provide either an outside, hose-yourself, or an inside on-site shower. It's always refreshing just to get that clean water on you, add some soap, scrub everywhere, clean, and put on dry clothes; then you're good to go. So much fun!

What about being clean ***inside?*** Not as easy.

In Matthew 23:25-27, Jesus taught us about cleanliness.

> *"Woe to you, teachers of the law and Pharisees, you hypocrites! You clean the outside of the cup and dish, but inside they are full of greed and self-indulgence. Blind Pharisee! First clean the inside of the cup and dish, and then the outside also will be clean. Woe to you, teachers of the law and Pharisees, you hypocrites! You are like whitewashed tombs, which look beautiful on the outside but on the inside are full of the bones of the dead and everything unclean." (Matthew 23:25-27).*

I remember the training we had to do to be able to participate in these kinds of races, and the food choices we had to make to be able to keep our bodies healthy and build the stamina to succeed and enjoy such activities at the same time. At the end of the day, it's not that important because Jesus taught us that the Christian life is lived from the inside out.

> *"Don't you see that whatever enters the mouth goes into the stomach and then out of the body? But the things that come out of a person's mouth* ***come from the heart,*** *and these defile them. For out of the heart come evil thoughts—murder, adultery, sexual immorality, theft, false testimony, slander. These are what defile a person; but eating with unwashed hands does not defile them." (Matthew 15:17-20).*

It's not about the races, nor the food to eat. I have to remind myself that what I do to myself—soul, body, and mind—is to glorify the Lord. As an expression of my thankfulness, an awe that His love is unfathomable, mind-blowing, that He made us in His image.

> *"So God created mankind in his own image, in the image of God he created them; male and female he created them." (Genesis 1:27).*

If you read that again, God created mankind. He is in us all! He created us in His own image. If you ask me who I would want to look like, I would pick any good-looking creature I see. What an honor it is that God gave us a gift and showed us that we are deserving of His image. So, take care of that body of yours.

"Do you not know that ***your bodies are temples of the Holy Spirit.***

> *"Do you not know that your bodies are temples of the Holy Spirit, who is in you, whom you have received from God? You are not your own; you were bought at a price. Therefore honor God with your bodies." (1 Corinthians 6:19-20).*

I am a work in progress. It's a continuous journey, an ongoing process of being refined from the inside out. It's not just about outward change, but about the deep, quiet work happening within. The pruning of pride, the shedding of old wounds, the surrender of hidden struggles.

Every day, I'm learning what it means to be clean on the inside, to have a heart that chooses forgiveness over bitterness, peace over chaos, and humility over ego. Some days, I get it right. Other days, I miss the mark and fall short. But grace meets me in both.

> *"Watch and pray so that you will not fall into temptation. The spirit is willing, but the flesh is weak." (Matthew 26:41).*

Which reminds me of the passage from Galatians 5:17 about conflict: "For the flesh desires what is contrary to the Spirit, and the Spirit what is contrary to the flesh. They are in conflict with each other, so that you are not to do whatever you want."

The kind of cleaning isn't quick or easy. Oh, how I wish, it could be. It's a daily choice to let God search my heart, reveal what doesn't belong, and replace it with His truth. Healing takes time. Transformation takes surrender. But I'm not who I used to be, and I'm not yet who I am becoming.

So, I keep showing up. I let God do the inner work. I trust that every step forward, no matter how small, is progress because He's not done with me yet, and I'm thankful for that.

This is just a gift that keeps on giving. Not only do we look like His image, but also for the Holy Spirit to dwell in us? This only puts me on my knees, and I pray to the song "Sanctuary" by Randy Scruggs and John W. Thompson, adapted by Billy Jonas. Give it a listen, as it is a powerful hymn of understanding the Lord came to save us and asking Him to prepare our bodies to be sanctuaries for Him.

I wanna be a living sanctuary for You, Lord.

Reflection

True transformation starts in the heart because God doesn't want to change what's seen, but He also wants to heal what's hidden. When we invite God to cleanse us from the inside out, He doesn't just fix the surface; He renews our spirit. Let Him wash away what doesn't belong and make room for His holiness to shine through.

Questions

What areas of your heart are you holding back from God?

What might change if you fully let Him in to cleanse and renew you?

Gratitude

Lord, thank you for loving me as I am. I'm grateful for Your mercy that washes me clean and Your grace that renews my heart day by day. Amen.

23
Fishing Lessons

Funny how this topic came up just as my husband sent me a memory photo of our kids' first fishing trip. We had been invited to Georgia, where our aunt asked if we'd like to take the kids fishing.

"Sure!" I said—though I knew absolutely nothing about fishing. I like to eat fish, but fishing itself? Not exactly my first choice of activity.

When we arrived at the man-made pond—or maybe it was a lake—the kids wasted no time. Not even a minute passed before one of them caught a fish. Then another. And another. It went on like that for hours! The kids were thrilled, especially my son, and by the end of the day, they were already asking to go fishing again once we got home.

But fishing at home, in real waters, was an entirely different experience. Ten… fifteen minutes went by with no bites. Guess who ended up holding the line? Jim and I. The enthusiastic little "fisherman" had vanished. They couldn't understand why there were no fish biting. The excitement faded fast.

When we serve outside the church walls—through missions, charity work, or simple acts of kindness—we're stepping into our calling to be ***fishers of men.***

It is what our Lord said to His disciples.

> *"Come, follow me, Jesus said, and I will send you out to fish for people." (Matthew 4:19).*

Mission trips can feel like that stocked pond—full of energy, activity, and visible relationship building. But when we serve in "real waters," where the results aren't immediate or visible, will we drop our nets and walk away? Or will we listen to Jesus' voice saying…

> *He said, "Throw your net on the right side of the boat and you will find some. When they did, they were unable to haul the net in because of the large number of fish." (John 21:6).*

We often go to serve others but come home realizing we were the ones truly served. Jesus modeled this perfectly in Matthew 20:28.

> *"Just as the Son of Man did not come to be served, but to serve, and to give his life as a ransom for many." (Matthew 20:28).*

It's an honor to serve—whether across the world or right in our own towns. The truth is, your mission field is wherever you are.

What are you fishing for?

You don't need a passport to serve. Every cashier, coworker, patient, or neighbor is an opportunity to reflect the love of Jesus. A simple smile can brighten someone's day. A kind word can echo God's grace more than you realize.

Sometimes I think I'm out there to help others, but more often, I find that I'm the one being refined—shaped into who Jesus wants me to be. I may not be the most skilled fisherman, but Jesus is gracious. Every day is a new opportunity to cast the net—not just by speaking His Word, but by living it.

In Matthew 25:37-40, Jesus teaches us this.

> *"Then the righteous will answer him, 'Lord, when did we see you hungry and feed you, or thirsty and give you something to drink? When did we see you a stranger and invite you in, or needing clothes and clothe you? When did we see you sick or in prison and go to visit you? The King will reply, Truly I tell you, whatever you did for one of the least of these brothers and sisters of mine, you did for me." (Matthew 25:37-40).*

I haven't arrived—I'm still learning how to be Jesus to those around me. But I want to be available. I want to keep casting, even when the bites are few, knowing that God is working—in me, and through me.

Wanna be the fishers of men that follow Jesus.

Reflection

Serving others isn't about how many "fish" we catch—it's about obedience to the One who calls us to cast the net. Some days, the results will be visible and exciting. On other days, the waters will seem still and empty. But every act of service, done in love, ripples farther than we can see. God is always working beneath the surface.

Question

Where is God asking you to cast your net today? Are you willing to keep fishing, even when the results aren't immediate?

Prayer

Lord Jesus, thank you for calling me to be a fisher of men. Help me to stay faithful in casting the net You've given me—whether I see the catch or not. Teach me to serve with humility, love, and patience. Let my actions reflect Your heart, and may others see You through me. Amen.

24
I'm done...

"I'm done."

It's a phrase we hear countless times throughout the day. When a task is completed, that declaration carries excitement and accomplishment, a cheer, a smile, and a sense of pride.

I still remember one cute moment from when my kids were young (they will probably kill me for sharing this): the call to the bathroom, "I'm done!" Your parents know what that means…cleaning up follows.

But there's another way we use this phrase. In moments of challenge. At the height of storms. When we reach what feels like a dead end. I'm done" can become an expression of defeat—frustration, surrender, letting go can be the quicker and easier reaction.

God knows this experience. He created man in His own image (Genesis 1:27). After He created everything, He looked at His work and saw that it was good (Genesis 1:31). Yet Scripture tells us God's heart was deeply sorrowed and displeased with humanity's pervasive sinfulness, so He regretted and grieved He had made man (Genesis 6). And still, He loved us—enough to redeem us and adopt us as His children (Galatians 4:4-5). Time to clean up…

Even Jesus, fully God and fully human, knew frustration:

- *Disciples' unbelief (Mark 9:19, Matthew 16:5-11)*

- *Hardness of hearts (Mark 3:1-6)*
- *Anger at Sickness and Death (Mark 1:41, John 11)*
- *Hypocritical leaders, prioritizing religious rituals over human need (Matthew 23, Mark 3:4)*
- *Corruption in the temple (John 2:13-17, Matthew 21:12-13, Mark 11, Luke 21, Isaiah 56:7, Jeremiah 7:11)*
- *Children, the disciples looked down upon (Mark 10:14)*

Could you imagine if Jesus, in His frustration, had said, "I'm done?"

He had every right to. He could have looked at his disciples and said, "I've given you everything—direction, teaching, and example, yet you still don't get it."

But He didn't.

Instead, Jesus took on the task, fulfilling more than 300 prophecies with humility and obedience, never grumbling, even knowing:

He would be betrayed for thirty pieces of silver (Zechariah 11:12)—for Him, ***we are worth it***.

He would be crucified (John 3:14)—for Him, ***we are worth it***.

He would be pierced (Psalms 22:16)—for Him, ***we are worth it***.

He would die with the wicked, but be buried with the rich (Isaiah 53:9)—still***, we are worth it***.

Jesus completed every part of His mission. He gave us a model of forgiveness, empathy, patience, and love, reconciliation and healing—and left us a map for Kingdom living in the Beatitudes (Matthew 5:3-12).

- *Blessed are the poor in spirit, for theirs is the kingdom of heaven (v3)*
- *Blessed are those who mourn, for they will be comforted (v4)*
- *Blessed are the meek, for they will inherit the earth (v5)*
- *Blessed are those who hunger and thirst for righteousness, for they will be filled (v6)*
- *Blessed are the merciful, for they will be shown mercy (v7)*
- *Blessed are the pure in heart, for they will see God (v8)*
- *Blessed are the peacemakers, for they will be called children of God (v9)*
- *Blessed are those who are persecuted because of righteousness, for theirs is the kingdom of heaven (v10)*

There were many times in my own life when I said, "I'm done." I felt like a failure. Stubbornly, I would get back up and try again in my own strength—only to end up in the same place. Finally, I prayed and said, "I'm done."

And God's response blew me away.

"Good, now I can begin."

Time to clean up…

The end of your self-reliance may be the true beginning of your life in Christ. A kingdom purpose life.

When Jesus completed His work. He did not mock or brag. Instead, He prayed and asked the Father this.

> *"Jesus said, "Father, forgive them, for they do not know what they are doing." And they divided up his clothes by casting lots." (Luke 23:34).*

And then, with His final breath, He did *not declare that He was finished.* He declared...

It is finished...

Wanna be reliant on the Lord, knowing I must decrease so He will increase.

Reflection

When we say, "I'm done," it can either be an end in frustration or the beginning of surrender. Jesus could have given up on us, but He didn't. Instead, He showed us that true victory comes not from quitting, but from finishing with faithfulness. When we lay down our self-reliance and let God take over, that's where true life begins.

Question

Where in your life have you been saying, "I'm done" out of defeat, when God may be waiting for you to surrender and let Him begin?

Prayer

Lord, I confess that many times I have said, "I'm done" out of weariness and frustration. Forgive me for the moments I have tried to live in my own strength. Teach me to surrender fully to You, trusting that my end is truly the beginning of Your work in me. Thank you, Jesus, that You never gave up on us, but finished Your mission in love. Help me to walk in that same faithfulness today. In Jesus' name, Amen.

Conclusion

Not Yet Done

Turning over half a century seems so old. I have come to a season in my life where I thought by now, I'd have it figured out. The plans, the purpose, the calling—all in cruise control and neatly aligned. The truth is, I'm still working on my list of what I want to be when I grow up. As I align my life with Christ, I'm aligning to learn the purpose He has for me to complete His work for His kingdom.

I am grateful for every stage, every chapter, and every walk because if I were to list everything I'm thankful for, I probably wouldn't finish.

Storms have come, yes, but so have the rainbows. And every trial, every tear, every waiting moment was worth it.

"Tomorrow is never promised." James 4:13-15

Until then, there is work to be done.

"Faith without works is dead." James 2:26

There are dreams unfulfilled, gifts unused, and chapters unwritten. Time is flying more than we want to think. There's more to life, more to give, more to become.

"I must work the works of him who sent me while it is day (John 9:4), so that the man of God may be complete, equipped for every good work (2 Timothy 3:17), and whatever your hands find to do, do it with your might (Ecclesiastes 9:10). For it is God who works in you, to will and to act in order to fulfill his good purpose" (Philippians 2:13).

But what keeps me grounded is ***truth.*** The truth is that I am not behind, not forgotten, not finished. The truth is that God's timing is never late, and His purpose is never wasted. So I return to Paul's words in Philippians 4:8 and choose where to focus:

On what is ***true***, not on what I feel I've missed.

On what is ***noble***, not on regrets.

On what is ***pure and lovely***, even in a messy season.

On what is ***admirable and praiseworthy***, especially when I see God's fingerprints all over my life.

Because perspective shapes peace. And peace anchors purpose. And in God's hands, nothing—not even time—is ever lost.

I want to end with what I started.

Second Corinthians 5:17 says, "Therefore, if anyone is in Christ, he is a new creation: old things have passed away; behold, all things have become new."

Nothing is wasted when the purpose is to purely wanna be like Jesus.

Closing Prayer

> *"The LORD has done it this very day; let us rejoice today and be glad." (Psalms 118:24).*

Lord, thank you for weaving Your truth into every part of our lives, even the things we don't understand. Remind me that even in seasons of darkness, You are light. When life hits and feels like a tragedy, remind me of the cross and, more importantly, the empty tomb. Your brightness is expressed through the sun in the morning and the stars at night. Reminding me You are always near. Help me to see Your redemptive hand at work in the patterns of my life. Strengthen my faith, renew my hope, and draw me closer to Your heart. In Jesus's name. Amen.

Bibliography

Andolfo, I., Alper, S. L., and Iolascon, A. "Nobel Prize in Physiology or Medicine 2021, Receptors for Temperature and Touch: Implications for Hematology." *American Journal of Hematology* 97, no. 2 (February 1, 2022): 168–170. https://doi.org/10.1002/ajh.26407.

Ardiel, E. L., and Rankin, C. H. "The Importance of Touch in Development." *Paediatrics & Child Health* 15, no. 3 (March 2010): 153–156. https://doi.org/10.1093/pch/15.3.153.

Batterson, Mark. *The Circle Maker: Praying Circles Around Your Biggest Dreams and Greatest Fears.* Grand Rapids, MI: Zondervan, 2011.

Eckstein, M., Mamaev, I., Ditzen, B., and Sailer, U. "Calming Effects of Touch in Human, Animal, and Robotic Interaction—Scientific State-of-the-Art and Technical Advances." *Frontiers in Psychiatry* 11 (November 4, 2020): 555058. https://doi.org/10.3389/fpsyt.2020.555058.

Francis Chan. *The Cost of Discipleship.* YouTube video, 42:16. Posted by CornerstoneSF, October 19, 2019. https://www.youtube.com/watch?v=kZq7n2yF2FQ.

Lombardi, Vince. "Quotes." *Vince Lombardi Official Site.* Accessed August 6, 2025. https://vincelombardi.com/quotes/.

Mammoth Cave National Park. *"Mammoth Cave." National Park Service.* Last modified June 10, 2024. https://www.nps.gov/articles/mammothcave.htm.

Oxford University Press. "Good Morning, int. & n." In *Oxford English Dictionary.* Accessed August 6, 2025. https://doi.org/10.1093/OED/3688942903.

Origin and History of Good Morning. In *Etymonline.* Accessed August 6, 2025. https://www.etymonline.com/search?q=good+morning.

Wong, Hosanna. *Spoken Word.* Hosanna Wong, 2017. https://www.hosannawong.com/spokenword.

Footnotes

(Chicago Notes System)

1. *Batterson, Mark. The Circle Maker; Praying Circles around Your Biggest Dreams and Greatest Fears. Grand Rapids, MI: Zondervan, 2011.*
2. *Wong, Hosanna. Spoken Word. 2017. https://www.hosannawong.com/spokenword*
3. *M. Eckstein, I. Mamaev, B. Ditzen, and U. Sailer, "Calming Effects of Touch in Human, Animal, and Robotic Interaction—Scientific State-of-the-Art and Technical Advances,"* Frontiers in Psychiatry *11 (November 4, 2020): 555058. https://doi.org/10.3389/fpsyt.2020.555058.*
4. *E. L. Ardiel and C. H. Rankin, "The Importance of Touch in Development,"* Paediatrics & Child Health *15, no 3 (March 2010): 153-56. https://www.google.com/url?q=https://pmc.ncbi.nlm.nih.gov/articles/PMC2865952*
5. *I. Andolfo, S. L. Alper, and A. Iolascon, "Nobel Prize in Physiology or Medicine 2021, Receptors for Temperature and Touch: Implications for Hematology,"* American Journal of Hematology *97, no. 2 (February 1, 2022): 168–170, https://doi.org/10.1002/ajh.26407.*
6. *Lombardi, Vince. "Quotes." Vince Lombardi Official Site. Accessed October 2, 2025. https://vincelombardi.com/quotes/*
7. *Hall, John E.* Guyton and Hall Textbook of Medical Physiology. *14th ed. Philadelphia: Elsevier, 2021.*
8. *Hall, John E.* Guyton and Hall Textbook of Medical Physiology. *14th ed. Philadelphia: Elsevier, 2021.*
9. *Chan, Francis. "Pastor Francis Chan's Powerful Weekend in Prison | Testimony & Reflection."* YouTube Video, *18;47. Published November 16, 2018. https://www.youtube.com/watch?v=655YogpBYqY*
10. *Oxford University Press, "Good Morning, int. & n.," in* Oxford English Dictionary, *accessed August 6, 2025, https://doi.org/10.1093/OED/3688942903.*
11. *9.* Origin and History of Good Morning, *in* Etymonline, *accessed August 6, 2025, https://www.etymonline.com/search?q=good+morning.*
12. *Mammoth Cave National Park, "Mammoth Cave,"* National Park Service, *last modified June 10, 2024, https://www.nps.gov/articles/mammothcave.htm.*

About The Author

Marivic "Vic" Gillooley began a deeper, life-changing relationship with Christ at the age of 32. Born in the Philippines and now a seasoned nurse with over 30 years of experience, Vic has dedicated her life to caring for others, both physically and spiritually. She is a blessed wife to her husband, Jim, and has been graciously given the gift of a beautiful blended family with five children and cherished grandchildren.

Vic's love for learning fuels her passion for travel and adventure, always seeking new experiences and fresh revelations from God along the way. Purely Wanna Be is her first devotional book, born from her personal journey of faith, grace, and transformation — a heartfelt offering to encourage others to walk boldly and humbly with Christ.

www.ingramcontent.com/pod-product-compliance
Lightning Source LLC
LaVergne TN
LVHW010931110826
845149LV00013B/2540

* 9 7 8 1 9 6 0 6 4 1 9 6 0 *